STO

STORE

STO

27

Innocents Lost

Innocents Lost

When Child Soldiers Go to War

Jimmie Briggs

BASIC BOOKS

A Member of the Perseus Books Group
New York

Published by Basic Books,
A Member of the Perseus Books Group

Books published by Basic Books are available at special discounts for bulk purchases in the United States by corporations, institutions, and other organizations. For more information, please contact the Special Markets Department at the Perseus Books Group, 11 Cambridge Center, Cambridge, MA 02142, or special.markets@perseusbooks.com

A CIP catalog record for this book is available from the Library of Congress.

ISBN-13 978-0-465-00798-1
ISBN 0-465-00798-8

05 06 07 08 / 10 9 8 7 6 5 4 3 2 1

Contents

for Mariela

Foreword

OVER THE LAST SEVERAL YEARS a number of international initiatives have been undertaken to halt the practice of using children as soldiers. The United Nations Security Council has attempted to shame the forces engaged in this practice by publishing a list identifying them. As yet, however, these efforts have not had great consequence. Child soldiers are used in armed conflicts in more than twenty countries in various parts of the world. Often they are employed both by government forces and by guerillas battling them. At any given time, it is generally estimated, about three hundred thousand children—many girls as well as boys—are employed in armed conflict.

Jimmie Briggs has deepened our understanding of this terrible phenomenon by seeking out children in some of these conflicts, telling their stories and the stories of their families and their communities, and enabling us to see the national and international political context that shapes their destinies. An important feature of his research is his examination of the efforts that are made in some places—but not enough overall—to rescue children from coerced military service and to provide them with assistance in reestablishing an approximation of normal lives.

In bringing us face to face with the young people who have been child soldiers, Jimmie Briggs performs an important public service. He helps us to realize that, no matter the terrible crimes in which many of them have participated, they are children who share much in common with our own children. In this way he may light the fire needed for effective measures to halt the recruitment of children—generally by force—for armed combat.

It is not a problem without a solution. The international agreements and the shaming lists are steps in the right direction, but many more are required. The UN Security Council could prohibit the supply of weapons to governments and guerilla forces that use child soldiers. This could be followed by the publication of lists of countries supplying such weapons. If the Lord's Resistance Army, the bizarre guerilla force that has devastated northern Uganda for two decades, is immune to denunciations of its use of child soldiers, it is possible that the countries from which it purchases weapons are more susceptible to stigma.

So-called smart sanctions, such as travel bans on leaders of governments and armed forces employing child soldiers, or freezes on their assets abroad, could also be effective. Perhaps the most useful method of curbing the practice would be international criminal prosecution of those responsible. The former president of Liberia, Charles Taylor, has been indicted by the Special Court for Sierra Leone for recruiting child soldiers, as have other defendants before that court. (Indeed, David Crane, the American military lawyer who serves as chief prosecutor for that tribunal, which is jointly sponsored by the United Nations and the government of Sierra Leone, early on manifested his seriousness in addressing the problem of child soldiers by appointing a specialist in children's rights to his staff.)

The problem of child soldiers could also be addressed on a global level by the new International Criminal Court. Though it lacks jurisdiction over many of the forces that use child soldiers because their governments have not ratified the treaty for the court, that problem could be solved if the Security Council were to confer it with jurisdiction.

In exploring the issue of reintegration of former child soldiers into their families and communities, Jimmie Briggs may also help to mobilize more international support for such programs. If the measures taken up to now have done little to prevent the enlistment of children in armed conflict, the least that can be done is to assist those who manage to escape or who bring an end to their service in some other way. Neglecting them after they have been taught to kill compounds the tragedy of their lives and, most likely, helps to ensure that they pose a continuing threat to the lives of others.

—Aryeh Neier
President, Open Society Institute
January 2005

Preface

CHILDREN'S PARTICIPATION IN ARMED CONFLICT around the world is a huge challenge for national governments, peacemaking and peacekeeping forces, and humanitarian organizations, yet a nearly invisible one. Even in the most intense media coverage of a war, the children who are affected receive the least amount of attention. The tragedy of child soldiers is hidden in plain sight.

Youth are attractive to many military commanders throughout the world because they can be easily trained to carry out the most repulsive orders, they are able to tote most of today's lightweight weapons, and they can be found in abundance when adult males become scarce. The sad truth is that, under the right circumstances, children are capable of the most horrific acts.

Several years ago I picked up a copy of the *New York Times* to find an all-too-familiar image staring back at me. In a front-page color photograph a Liberian gunman knelt in a city street, howling in anger while pointing an automatic rifle at the photographer who captured his image. More chilling than the weapon he held was what he wore on his back: a pink teddy-bear backpack, a telling symbol of his lost youth. The phenomenon of children in combat is not recent, nor is it solely an issue in African countries, as many may assume. Children as young as eight years old are being used as soldiers, scouts, cooks, and sexual servants in mostly internal conflicts, from Uganda and Afghanistan to Sri Lanka and Colombia. This is a human rights violation issue just as deserving of attention as AIDS, refugee displacement, and economic disparity.

It wasn't until 1996 that the issue of children and war became a serious international concern. Graça Machel, a former first lady of Mozambique and eventual wife of Nelson Mandela, was asked by the United Nations Secretary-General to do a study examining the subject with the assistance of UN agencies and non-governmental organizations. Simply titled "Impact of Armed Conflict on Children," the report graphically documented the ways in which children—defined as younger than eighteen by international humanitarian law—were exploited by adults in conflict. Popularly known as the Machel Report, it created a harrowing portrait of millions of children succumbing to sickness, displacement, and orphanhood because of war. It also revealed that more than 250,000 kids were actively fighting in conflicts around the world, most under the age of fifteen.

At the time of the study's release, more than two million children under eighteen had been killed and another six million seriously injured or permanently disabled by armed conflict in the previous decade. On its recommendation, UN Secretary-General Kofi Annan created the position of Special Representative to the Secretary-General on Children and Armed Conflict, selecting Olara Otunnu, a native Ugandan diplomat, to fill the office.

Some would argue that America has its own problem with child "fighters" who carry guns as members of gangs or drug rings. But more often than not, those young people have some alternatives for escape, as well as institutions that can help them. But in other countries where children have taken up arms, voluntarily or by force, there has been a breakdown in society, making the youngsters vulnerable to war's abuses with daunting odds of escape.

Photographers have taken countless pictures of children holding guns, but who has come forward to demand how or why they have the weapons? Who has invaded a country or imposed sanctions because children there are being used as soldiers or are targeted for violence, displacement, or trauma? There's a popular saying among journalists that the first casualty of war is the truth. I disagree. It's always the children.

The six-year journey of writing this book has been about seeking to understand how children can be drawn into war and what it does to them and their communities. But the idea for this book began not with a child, but with a dying woman whom I met on my first trip to Rwanda in 1998. I still wake up at night sometimes with my own silent screams in the belief that I killed her, just as sure as if my hand had pulled a trigger or plunged a knife through her heart. I see her face when I wake or during a furtive moment walking along a buzzing avenue. She is a reminder of every housing project, drug-infested street corner, and scarred village I ever entered and left as a journalist without a backward glance.

Three years after the genocide in Rwanda, I went to the central African nation of Congo, then known as Zaire, with the intention of reporting a civil war. Instead, I discovered the unshakable guilt borne by all survivors or witnesses of human tragedy—not really survivor's guilt, but more like "witness guilt."

British photographer Derek Hudson and I were traveling with a local driver and French television crew. We'd arrived in Kisangani in the northeastern section of the country aboard a United Nations–chartered airplane one morning in late March. En route from Goma, a border town between the Democratic Republic of Congo and Rwanda, I couldn't help staring at the preteen boys holding up rifles taller than they were. They were fighting on behalf of the rebel forces challenging the government based in the capital of Kinshasa. Some had relatively mundane duties—serving as guards, carrying the bags of their adult commanders, or working in kitchens. Many more saw frontline combat, erasing all but the bare vestiges of their childhoods with each round fired from their AK–47s. With their too-large uniforms, slight builds, and smooth faces, they could have been youngsters playing a game of war. But the vacant look in their eyes was that of old soldiers.

The refugees we encountered in Kisangani were even more lost than the boy soldiers of Goma. Adrift since their own nation's bloody tumult several years before, a mass of Rwandan Hutus were stranded by a civil war between the regime of strongman Mobutu Sese Seko and insurgents led by Laurent Kabila. Most of the Rwandans were now in the jungle between Kisangani and Ubundu to the south. The farther one got from Kisangani, the more desperate the situation became. At its worst the death toll among the refugees was two hundred a day from starvation, cholera, or murder. The road leading to the refugees' location from Kisangani wasn't a road at all but a muddied, washed-out path lined with mud-brick homes, huts, and lean-tos. Thousands of people lined the route. Their tattered clothing, bare feet, and emaciated forms blended together, making women and men, young and old, indistinguishable. There were no graves. The dead and the living shared the same ground. The line between the two states itself seemed blurred.

"She's dead, isn't she?" I asked no one in particular, slowly walking toward a figure lying by the side of the road. A small form covered with a patterned wool blanket rested on a bamboo stretcher. I assumed the refugee was a woman, but given the expression on what remained of a face, I couldn't be sure. The tall, lanky soundman turned and whispered, "She's alive." At that moment I heard the moan. The cameraman and a still photographer leaned in to capture their images. I moved in for a closer look.

"Uuunh," came the sound again. The color was already leaving the body, giving her skin a greyish cast. She didn't move once, and that scared me the most. The only sounds were the constant moaning and the nervous shifting of our feet. The jungle gave us nothing to hear. It didn't have to. Through its most vicious minions it had begun processing its claim on her. Dozens of ants and flies were venturing in and out of the deaf ears, sightless eyes, and open, unmoving mouth. Standing on that muddy stretch of road in the largest country in Africa, I understood that the most violent things done to the human body are by the earth's smallest creatures.

Were we going to take her somewhere? How much longer did she have? Should we put her out of her misery? These were questions that none of us spoke aloud, but I know we all thought them. Never having watched someone literally be eaten alive, I stubbornly fought back tears so the others wouldn't see my weakness. The next few minutes seemed like hours as one by one we turned and walked back to the truck. The decision had been made without a word being said: We were going to leave her to die. I walked a few steps ahead of the others and found my lips involuntarily forming the words to the Lord's Prayer. My insides were hollow for having become a silent partner in the decision to let another person die that day.

Slamming the doors shut, we focused our eyes on a point beyond comprehension as the vehicle lurched forward. The moaning slowly grew distant. As we retreated from the jungle, I could feel only remorse. A man in a clerical collar came up to us and asked if I would help his ailing wife and children. Watching the children play on a strip of railroad track, all I could do was smile and say, "We're journalists, but we'll be back. There's nothing to give now." Even as I said it, I suspected I would never see him again. By the look on his face, so did he.

This journey to explore the lives of child soldiers and war-affected children was my way of "going back." Across three continents and six years I struggled, mostly against myself, to complete it in the hope of reaching an understanding about why children are drawn into conflict and how the vicious process could be stopped. On one of my first trips, to Uganda, someone in the strife-torn area of Gulu told me, "If a dying man tells you his story, there's an obligation to pass it on." This book is my attempt not only to tell their stories but also to make people care enough to do something about this scourge. More than any other natural resource or commodity, childhood is the most valuable asset a society can maintain. War never fails to destroy it, whether a child is facing or holding a weapon.

1

The Unforgiven:
The Children of Genocide in Rwanda

EVERYDAY LIFE IS FULL OF CHOICES, and they only grow more complicated with age, as do the consequences. Few people are forced to make life-and-death choices, especially in their youth. Yet in the spring of 1994, sixteen-year-old François Minani was confronted with a choice that, had it occurred anywhere but Rwanda, one might have thought unimaginable. What happened to François and his family on that fateful day was tragically repeated thousands of times throughout the central African nation.

François lived with his parents, John and Valerie, on a small hillside plot in the mountainous community of Gitarama. Like many teenagers in his area, he'd stopped his education after elementary school and worked with his father and extended family, growing cassava, beans, and yams. On the morning of May 11, another teen from the Bugoba section of Gitarama came to François's home leading a band of youth. His name was

Uwimana, and he ordered Valerie to bring François and her four grandchildren and follow him. The four small boys—Buregeya, Mukamurigo, Mukarukundo, and Mukashyaka—were the children of François's older sister, Mukakabera.

Fearful, François, his mother, and the grandchildren went with Uwimana up the hill. They passed Rose Bankundiye and her daughter Musabimana working on their vegetable patch. They passed the home of Rutagerura, whose son Protais silently watched the procession go by. Finally they reached a shallow pit and presented to François and his mother a heart-stopping choice.

"Give us five thousand francs, and we will kill your daughter's children," Uwimana told Valerie. "Otherwise, François will do it for us."

"My son is not a killer," she shot back.

"Then we will teach him," came the matter-of-fact reply.

Overcome with horror, Valerie turned and left for home. François's captors then handed him two things: narcotics to numb his mind and senses and a hoe to use on his terrified nephews. François Minani was the son of a Tutsi mother and Hutu father. A Hutu-led genocide against Tutsis had been unfolding across the nation for over a month, and François had to prove where his allegiances lay. His sister was already dead, as was her Tutsi fiancé. Now it was their children's turn. Looking down into the grave, already filling with bodies of neighbors and relatives he'd known his whole life, François froze. One of Uwimana's followers started beating him with a stick. Finally, he took the hoe and crushed each of his nephew's skulls, throwing their limp corpses down into the hole with their mother's. He would recall their eyes staring up at him in disbelief as each blow was struck.

When it was done, he was allowed to leave, and he trudged back home. The horror of his actions weighed heavily. "It was a horrible thing," his family told him, "but you had no choice."

———

The journey of creating this book began and ended in Rwanda. I was a journalist for *Life* magazine when I started it, and I had been in a position to report on a diverse range of interesting stories. But nothing, absolutely nothing, could have prepared me for what I saw and heard in Rwanda in early 1997.

Over the span of a hundred days three years before, one of the most brutal events of the twentieth century had unfolded in a country the size of New Hampshire. Rwanda had withstood decades of civil strife—a legacy of colonial rule and influence, a textbook case of divide and conquer. In 1959, the majority Hutu population overthrew the ruling Tutsi king. Three years later the country gained its independence from Belgium. During the next several years thousands of minority Tutsis were killed, and another 150,000 went into exile. Exiles and their children formed the Rwandan Patriotic Front (RPF), a group that began a resilient insurgency in 1990. The war and other constant political and economic crises exacerbated ethnic tensions. On April 6, 1994, Juvenal Habyarimana, the Rwandan president who had led a Hutu-dominated government for two decades, was killed in a plane crash at the national airport in the capital of Kigali. The Hutus instigated their campaign of terror against the Tutsis the following day.

Within hours of the incident, which many Rwandans and international observers suspected wasn't accidental, roving bands of Hutu militia known as "Interhamwe" invaded cities and rural communes exhorting Hutus to kill. In scenes reminiscent of the film *Apocalypse Now*, with bloodied corpses strewn on the ground, neighbors turned on each other with cutting tools. Machetes were the weapons of choice, but panga sticks—wooden clubs with nails or spikes—were also used. Families, neighbors, and coworkers who had existed alongside each other for years now turned on one another in a murderous rampage. According to Human Rights Watch, thousands of Tutsi

3

women were raped or sexually assaulted, leading to the births of thousands of children, known as *enfants mauvais souvenirs*, "the children of bad memories."[1]

People were burned alive or butchered in their homes. Women were gang-raped and mutilated with farm tools. Churches, normally safe havens in times of conflict and disaster, became bloody morgues as members of the predominantly Catholic clergy allowed murderers inside. Millions of Tutsis fled into neighboring Tanzania, Zaire, and Kenya. The national radio station, RTLM, broadcasted lists of the dead and encouraged people to especially target the "cockroaches," the Tutsi children who could grow up to become adults seeking revenge.

During one of a handful of trips I made to Rwanda over a seven-year period, a Tutsi Rwandan survivor told me, "Until the last survivor has died, there will be no forgiveness for what happened." The thousands of Hutu children and youth who participated were not exempt and would have to shoulder the burden through adulthood as the unforgiven bearers of the genocide's horror.

In April 2004, I returned to Rwanda for my fourth and final visit during the nation's commemoration of the tenth anniversary of the genocide. I'd come to visit François Minani, the teen who'd killed his nephews in Gitarama, as well as see how the country was faring ten years after the genocide. On the second day of the trip, I made a trip to Kibuye, two hours west of Kigali, the capital.

Early one morning I saw a small group of men working silently behind the maternity ward of Kibuye Hospital. A steadily growing bunch of pregnant women amassed nearby. Under the shade of a guava tree, the men stood around a shallow pit of soft earth as two or three at a time took turns swinging with shovels and pickaxes. It was an excavation site that quickly widened like a pool of blood. The mass grave yielded rock, odd pieces of metal, empty food cans, but no bodies.

Nearby a solemn man in slacks and a track-suit jacket stood with his arms folded, watching intently. During the genocide he'd been working in the hospital's surgical ward when a young girl came in, bloodied from being slashed with machetes. For hours he worked alone tending her severe wounds. She was conscious, alive, and for him that was enough to have hope. It wouldn't last long, though, because the killers came right into the unit where he was working. Helplessly he watched them drag her behind the hospital. The grave had already been dug, and she was thrown in alive, breathing and watching. The man didn't know how many other victims joined her in the following hours and days, but he had come on that day to guide the searchers with a need to find the girl he almost saved.

I was accompanied by photographer Damaso Reyes. After leaving the diggers at the hospital still searching for bodies, we drove up into the misty, lush green hills overlooking Lake Kivu, bordering the Democratic Republic of Congo. Unlike their counterparts at the hospital, the men we found digging on one hill came upon bodies in short order. They were working on a shallow grave, and the bodies had been buried head to toe in a line that extended along a culvert and down the hill. The remains were excavated and laid alongside the long, narrow pit. Their condition left the gruesome details of the deaths to little imagination. The bones of adult men and women, as well as the tiny remains of children, were recovered, some broken in chunks, others shattered to tiny slivers. The diggers, their faces set hard and expressionless, methodically stacked split ribs and skulls detached from spines in neat piles.

In eerie silence, the men took turns breaking up the wet earth with shovels and pickaxes. Soiled, disintegrated clothing was separated from the remains and placed in a heap nearby. Their foreheads and sinewy arms glistened with sweat in the humid air as a small crowd of onlookers quickly grew from half a dozen to more than twenty. Most of the assembled were children, too young to remember what had happened. As the digging continued, their innocent eyes held curious gazes. After two hours six bodies were unearthed. Halfway through the effort, one of the onlookers shouted, "That's Easter!" A digger had retrieved a victim whose remains were miraculously intact. The skull was wrapped in a red-and-white rosary with several links missing. The arms were folded and held what appeared to be a small, brown burlap sack. Inside the bag was the decomposed body of a small child wearing a shirt and pants. "That was her son," whispered the same man.

Damaso, Raymond, a Rwandan producer for CNN, and I watched, filmed, and photographed much of the digging. Our emotions mirrored those of the native onlookers. "Where was Jesus when this happened?" asked Damaso, an avowed atheist, nearly spitting out the question. Raymond was silent. I stared down at the ragged grave, creating a boundary between us and the people living on the hill. Partly obscured by a thin white mist, Lake Kivu shimmered a beautiful dull blue several hundred feet below. The contrast of the inviting water and the torn, red earth in which we stood was not lost on me. "Perhaps God had been here all along, keeping the memory of what happened here alive," I thought silently, "for us to bear witness."

While the focus of this book is on children who participate in war, it is also about the other victims who happen to be young. It is impossible to explore the lives of kids carrying guns in conflict without seeing those who've been displaced, orphaned, denied access to education, or directly victimized, sexually or otherwise. They're all victims, and the barriers separating them are tenuous. As the 1996 Machel Report and organizations such as the London-based Coalition to Stop the Use of Child Soldiers point out, it is the least protected children who are most vulnerable to recruitment or coercion into armed struggle. If one hopes to understand who "child soldiers" are, then one has to look at all these children.

The legacy bestowed on Rwanda's children since the 1994 genocide has been its biggest struggle. Children were targets and perpetrators to an unprecedented degree. Just as the formal institutions of its society—such as the judicial, medical, and educational—were targeted and destroyed in the genocide, so was the very notion of childhood. According to the Rwandan government, UNICEF, and international relief agencies such as the International Rescue Committee (IRC), approximately one million children are considered "vulnerable," meaning they are at risk of being displaced from their homes, not attending school, being exploited, living in poverty, or contracting diseases. Unfortunately, not even the state authorities know where all of these youth are living.

In the decade after the genocide, several hundred thousand children were forced to survive without one or both parents. The phenomenon is the result of parental deaths during the genocide and the subsequent repatriation of Hutus from surrounding countries, particularly the Congo, starting in 1996. The majority of today's children were not yet born when the genocide happened, but Rwanda's new generation of orphans, street kids, and young survivors of sexual violence may be among its most visible and tragic victims. Too often they are left to deal with its legacies of trauma, poverty, and HIV/AIDS alone. It's impossible to talk about someone like François Minani without considering the experience of a Clementine.

CLEMENTINE

A fourteen-year-old survivor during the genocide, Mukamutsime Clementine, along with her four brothers and sisters, hid in a grove of bushes during a Hutu rampage of their community. "We were with my father and his friend," Clementine recalled, sitting in the front room of the mud-brick home she shared with her siblings in Rwamagana, an hour east of Kigali. She pulled at the light-colored plaid dress she wore, while her eyes drifted toward the ceiling. "The killer saw my father's friend and ran towards him." Her father and his friend ran in one direction, Clementine and her siblings in another.

Deafening pellets of rain pounded the roof of corrugated steel and banana leaves when I spoke with Clementine, on a stormy afternoon after the killing stopped in 1998.

"Whump! Whump! Whump!" In a short time, streams of water were flowing through invisible gaps of the igloo-shaped structure. Sitting cross-legged on a woven mat, Clementine was visibly embarrassed and self-conscious about the leaks. Occasionally, she raised a hand to hold up her head, but most of the time her eyes were fixed on the packed dirt on the floor of the hut. She and two younger brothers shared two rooms separated by a thatched partition of bamboo and banana leaves. The front room was for cooking, with pots, gourds, and a small area for fire. In the living area where she sat, a wooden bench ran alongside the left wall. Clothes hung on a rope strung across a far wall.

The three kids were all that was left of a family of eleven. After separating from her father, Clementine and the two boys headed north to Uganda, attempting to reach a grandfather. En route, they were attacked by Interhamwe militiamen, and she was struck in the head with a machete. For weeks she lay unconscious in a field hospital; her brothers were taken to an orphanage. When she improved, the three were brought to the Fred Rwigema Unaccompanied Minors' Center in Rwamagana, established by local Rwandan authorities after the genocide to deal with the overwhelming needs of abandoned youth.

In October 1994, the International Rescue Committee took over the center, which could accommodate 220 children. Unlike some centers in the period immediately after the genocide, Rwigema focused primarily on reuniting children with their families. In the five years after the genocide, its staff managed to connect 1,500 children to family members through photo and radio broadcast tracing.

The United Nations defines "unaccompanied children" as those under eighteen without parental or adult family member custody. This includes street children, prisoners, those in foster care, orphans, and youth in child-headed households. By the spring of 2004, there were twenty-four centers in Rwanda for so-called unaccompanied children, many fewer than even before the genocide (no one knows exactly how many there were then). In 1997, the government instituted a "one child, one family" policy to place orphans or unaccompanied children with foster families or in community care. The traditional response for children without identified relatives was to house them in centers, but thankfully that attitude changed.

After two years at Rwigema, Clementine and her brothers were found by relatives who took them to their grandfather. He'd been found by IRC's Rwigema team.

"We would receive food and clothing, but he took them for his other children," said Clementine of her grandfather, a Baptist minister. "I wanted to go to secondary school, but he wouldn't pay. So I had no choice but to leave. To go to school means everything."

The young teenager walked hundreds of miles from Uganda back to the land in Rwanda that her family had owned before the genocide. Once she had established a home and was sure she could find work, she went back for her brothers.

When we met, only her youngest brother was in school. Clementine farmed beans for money and daily food; beans along with banana stalk was the typical meal.

"I can do what I can for us," she told me, holding her head down and pulling at her long, dingy dress. "I go to church every week to sing in the choir. God got me through this." At the very least, she and her brothers had a home. By 2004, there were seven thousand homeless youth struggling throughout Rwanda, half in Kigali alone.

About one-third of these wayward youths were "socioeconomic" cases. They had families and might even go to a home in the evenings but did not attend school. They roamed the streets of Rwanda's capital from dawn to dusk, hunting for any form of subsistence or money. At night, they might go home, return to a shelter, or find uneasy rest behind a garbage bin.

In February 2003, the IRC developed a strategy for integrating street kids. Eight centers for street children were built in Kigali. The organization focused on providing technical support to the staff to help them reintegrate kids into the community. The plan also provided a public, decentralized place for street children to meet daily. Each child would have a profile developed to track them.

Even if children at these transit centers and other institutions, as well as kids returning home at night, are included, estimated numbers of unaccompanied children were probably too low. In the capital, police had regular roundups in which kids were taken off the streets and placed in centers in other parts of the country. Unfortunately, the youths were not given individual case files in an initial police action, so authorities had no way of tracking them or assessing their individual needs. Genocide orphans were thrown in with economic hardship cases and AIDS sufferers indiscriminately. More often than not, the youths managed to make it back to their regular street haunts in short time.

In 1998, I visited Project Rafiki in a rural area just outside Kigali. A center described by many observers as a success, Rafiki sat on about thirty acres of private land, nestled among green hills and thick woods. Children stayed there six to eight months at a time and then were sent to foster homes, back to the streets, or, if possible, to a home of their own. Having managed to trace eighty families for youths who came there, the project housed approximately 150 children between the ages of eight and seventeen—about twenty of them girls—when I went to visit. Others came in the daytime and returned to Kigali at night to work outside the city's nightclubs and restaurants. They were called "carwashers."

Life on the street meant risking diseases such as malaria, diarrhea, respiratory infection, and AIDS. But as one Rafiki staffer said to me, "After the genocide, what is AIDS?"

The center sought to deal with the day-to-day struggles of the young people surviving alone on the streets, offering everything from safe-sex lectures to career counseling. Further, children could learn how to read and write in Swahili, French, English, and Kinyarwanda, as well as develop highly desirable skills such as carpentry and electrical work.

"We try to do a parallel between the life they had on the streets and their lives now," explained Ahmedi, a staffer who'd once been homeless. "We pick up kids from the street one day and take them back the next. No one is forced to stay at the center. The decision is theirs."

CELESTINE

Celestine was a young man who'd made the decision to leave the streets and gamble on a better life. For six years every day of survival without a home had been a small victory. His mother died in the genocide, and after his father took a new wife with whom Celestine constantly fought, the ten-year-old went to the streets of Kigali. "The first challenge was finding somewhere to eat, then somewhere to sleep," he recalled to me. "You could never find a good place to sleep at night. During the night, you had to struggle for food because it would be taken. You had to fight."

"The police say they do roundups because of security, which may or may not be true," explained Marie Louise Uwineza, coordinator of Volet: Enfants de la Rue-CPAJ, a transit center for street kids sponsored by the

Presbyterian Church of Rwanda. Located in Kucikoro, a neighborhood on the outskirts of Kigali, CPAJ also received assistance from Catholic Relief Services and Handicap International. Since opening its doors in 1998, the center had assisted five thousand boys and girls, making it one of the success stories about street children. During the genocide the area was heavily populated with Tutsis, so losses were extremely high. "The problem with kids surviving on the streets was so big after the war," said Uwineza. "Some of the kids we were seeing had parents killed or raped, leaving them with HIV or AIDS." CPAJ was a transit center, which means kids were not housed at its facility, at least not in large numbers. The small staff of eight worked with the surrounding community to place kids in homes or find places for older youths to share living space.

"We want the kids to be living in the community, rather than at the center," explained Uwineza. "If possible, a child and surviving relatives are identified and reunited, or we introduce kids into the area." Of the 150 kids coming for assistance, about forty-five stayed at the center on occasion. There were vocational programs for the youth to learn candle-making, furniture-building, postcard and T-shirt design, as well as baking. After six months of this professional training, the youth in the individual classes were organized into mini-professional associations, and CPAJ provided seed funding and set them up with government work. Students attending secondary school and university had their fees covered as well.

Celestine was one former street kid who'd been coming to CPAJ for three years. When I met him, he was a secondary-school student living with another former street youth in a house. "At first, when I was in the dustbin, I didn't know how to speak English, obey people, or wash clothes," he told me. "Now, I have the knowledge to separate the good and the bad. In my future I want to do something with technology, putting things together."

The "dustbin" is not just a metaphor. It is the mammoth Kigali trash dump located a bumpy ten-minute ride from CPAJ. "The center was intentionally built here so we could have access to the young people," explained Uwineza. The dump sat atop a muddy, craggy hill against a backdrop of lush green mountains. "We're constantly trying to get the kids at the dustbin to the center, but many of them are high on marijuana, glue, or cigarettes," she noted. "They don't want to give up their freedoms by coming to us."

A few miles away from the center, several dozen children sifted through stinking mounds of refuse across a pockmarked patch of mud and grass. On a breezy, humid afternoon, Mary Louise Uwineza escorted Damaso and me on a brief tour of the dump. Flies swarmed incessantly, but the youth, dressed in tattered clothing and mismatched shoes, seemed oblivious. "They develop their own immunities," explained Uwineza.

Surrounding the fields of human waste, broken furniture, and food scraps were large green containers. When the rain fell heavy, the young people slept inside of them. There was one small girl searching for scraps of potatoes. She was the only female among the group of older boys. Her name was Chantal, and she had gone to the dump every day for the last four years. Like most of them, she was not homeless but lived with her mother and younger siblings in a nearby shanty. Her father had died in the genocide, and, never having gone to school a day in her life, Chantal cared for her family by scrounging for food and charcoal with which to cook it. She took a few minutes to explain her story and allow pictures to be taken then returned to a small mass of trash to dig with a stake, and her hands if necessary. "This," observed Uwineza sadly, "is her everyday job."

Girls and women unarguably fared the worst in the genocide. As Hutu attackers murdered and pillaged across the Rwandan countryside, over a quarter of a million girls and women were raped and sexually assaulted. The attacks were not just with male organs but with sticks, machetes, pipes, and other inanimate objects. In the years since that time, between half a million and a million Rwandans tested positive for HIV or AIDS. Among the several thousand children who were born from the rapes, a number of them were given away or abandoned to the streets. These were *enfants mauvais souvenirs.*

"It was difficult for the raped women to accept these children into their families," observed Dr. Odette Nyiramilimo, "but they eventually did over time. Abortion is not accepted in Rwanda. Even doctors who do it cannot admit it. It's considered 'an understanding between doctors.' The women who delivered these children would tell me, 'I lost all my other family and children; at least I have one. This is a gift from God.'"

Nyiramilimo was a senator in the Rwandan parliament and chairperson of a legislative committee dealing with social affairs and human rights. Previously, she was cabinet minister for social affairs. An ob-gyn by training and a Tutsi, Dr. Nyiramilimo operated one of the few medical clinics specifically providing services to women victimized during the genocide. She saw those who'd been infected with disease, borne children, or been severely traumatized. She herself had not been sexually assaulted, but Dr. Nyiramilimo was a major advocate for those women who were. "'You must seek justice,' I told the women," she recalled. "There are only one hundred thousand people in prison, but there are many, many who are free. They may never face justice. People start laughing and harass the women who make accusations of rape or sexual assault."

After the genocide ended, "for the first three months, it was a challenge for me to see people who could have been killers in the genocide enter the clinic. As a medical doctor, I had to give the appropriate attention and show them I was not afraid," she said. Nyiramilimo's emotional scars ran deep. All members of her extended family were killed in the genocide.

The only family she had left was her husband, their three children, and an adopted daughter. In providing desperately needed medical assistance, she found a form of therapy.

Sexuality is a taboo subject for public conversation in the conservative, predominantly Catholic nation. Out of the sixty-five thousand confessions by imprisoned defendants to genocidal crimes, only nine were to sexual violence by the spring of 2004. "After the genocide, there were a number of wounded patients, physically and morally, [and we were] without enough means to take care of them," explained Dr. Nyiramilimo. On my final trip to Rwanda in the spring of 2004, I met one woman-child who was the perfect example of such a survivor, a sad individual whose life had been destroyed more than the eye could see.

EUGENIE

The oldest daughter in a family of three children, Eugenie had been a virgin until Rwandan Hutu soldiers abducted her in Gitarama, Rwanda, in April 1994. Over a week's period, countless young men and boys took turns raping her in a wooded area. She could hear screams of death at a nearby church. Other civilians were being slaughtered on the sacred grounds where she had been headed. Chronologically twenty-six years old when I met her, Eugenie remained frozen as the sixteen-year-old teenager who lost her virginity, her hope, and nearly the will to live a decade before.

"We're not going to kill you," her abductors told the slight teenager. "We're going to take you as a wife."

When I spoke with her, she was a frail woman dressed in a plain gray blouse and skirt; her trembling hands clutched a small flowered purse as she told her story. It was on a rainy afternoon in the offices of AVEGA, a Rwandan NGO based in the capital of Kigali that assisted female survivors of sexual violence. Looking at her taut face and dull expression, I started to cry. Aurea, the woman translating from Kinyarwanda for me, smiled and leaned over to touch my arm.

"You're too sensitive," she said softly.

"No, I'm just tired," I replied wearily. "I've heard too many stories." At that point I'd recorded the experiences and thoughts of children around the world, and each story had started taking me further from home, further from my own cherished little girl, Mariela. Listening and watching Eugenie, I began seeing Mariela's face.

Her attackers made her repeat daily, "We Tutsis are like dogs. Our days are numbered." They violated her to the point where she was physically unable to escape, even when the opportunity presented itself. She lay like a corpse on forest branches and leaves, waiting for the next soldier to rape her. "When the RPF guerillas entered Gitarama, my attackers were scared," she recalled. "They told me I could go, because they wanted to escape themselves." But, she continued, "you are already dead. There's no life in front of you."

Before the genocide Eugenie was, as she described it, "whole." Her family was Tutsi and lived a modest life about thirty miles outside Kigali. They farmed sorghum, sweet potatoes, and cassava—the typical means of survival. Eugenie had three little brothers and a sister. Her father farmed, and her mother sold small handicrafts at a local market. Soon after the killing began, Eugenie's father disappeared. She never found out what happened to him. Her mother was murdered and stuffed into a toilet, she says. The killers tried to flush her, as a joke. The children dispersed to the homes of relatives.

"I ran away to my aunt's house," said Eugenie. "My aunt's neighbors told me to go away. 'You're not in that family,' they said. Finally, a [Hutu] militia came to the house, and my aunt took me to a neighbor. It was an old woman who told me to go [to] the church in Kabgayi."

Many Tutsi sought refuge in churches. Rwanda is a heavily Catholic nation because of its French and Belgian colonial influences. Eugenie believed she would be safe at the church. On her way there, armed men stopped her and asked for her identification card. She didn't have one, so she ran into a nearby forest to escape. The soldiers, members of the presidential guard, found her hiding in the trees.

After her ordeal at the hands of the Hutu men, RPF soldiers rescued her. She was taken to a hospital in an area called Muhango, past Gitarama, where she could finally "mend alone." Two years later, she found her siblings, who'd gone into hiding with friends and neighbors. In 2000, when she started going to AVEGA for assistance, they tested her for HIV. The results came back positive. With no surviving adult family members, she cared for her four younger siblings, all of whom are in their early to mid-teens. They lived in Kimironko Village, a community for women who are members of AVEGA.

Eugenie eventually was able to attend church services, but until a year before we met, she hadn't been able to—it brought back memories of the brutality she had endured within earshot of a church. In her late twenties, she's never had a boyfriend or considered getting married. "When I found out I had AIDS, it was like death," she lamented.

"When I'm not sick, I try to find something to do, to not think about the future. My brothers and sister know I have the disease. They know I will die, but they do not know about [her being attacked]." Because Eugenie took care of children, she received priority from AVEGA for antiviral medicine. Her strain of the disease had become resistant to the drugs, though, and her doctor wanted her to eat meat, milk, and eggs, but those foods are too expensive for her to afford on a daily basis.

"When I think about my life, what I want most is to go away and be alone," Eugenie said. "I don't want my brothers and sister to see my sadness. I can't show it. The rapists killed me; they broke me."

SURVIVAL AND TRAUMA

Juveniles essentially had four different roles in the genocide. First, some were members of the Interhamwe. Thousands of boys between fifteen and eighteen years old were part of the local militia. Several 1995 court cases in Kigali, for example, involved boys under eighteen years old who admitted to killing, many up to ninety civilians. Second, they were used as informants. Within the context of communal purges, the principal role of children was to identify Tutsi and moderate Hutu who were hiding from the Interhamwe, or local authorities. Youths also looted. Children of all ages and both sexes were involved in destroying houses and stealing personal property, including cattle and crops.

Finally, there were those considered to have been "associated" with the genocide. These were youths who were neither child soldiers nor participants in killing or looting, but who became associated with the Hutu army before, during, or after the flight of refugees into Zaire. Most of the associated youths were orphans who attached themselves to soldiers and their families in return for working as servants or guards.

The unparalleled mental trauma endured by survivors, particularly children, was an ongoing challenge for the Rwandan government and NGO community, even a decade after the killings had stopped. One relief worker described it to me as the highest level of child traumatization seen in the world. A survey of Rwandan youth done in 1996 showed that the overwhelming majority—90 percent of children—had seen someone beaten or killed in the genocide. Of three thousand minors between eight to nineteen interviewed, 80 percent had experienced the death of someone in the immediate family. As in most places affected by conflict, the most successful programs working with the mental health issues of children are those most culturally sensitive. Not every survivor—especially children—of conflict or disaster suffers from post-traumatic stress disorder, a common diagnosis after the Vietnam War era. Western approaches to healing and reconciliation do not always apply.

"Many children were traumatized during the war in 1994," noted Luc Chauvin, the director of UNICEF's advocacy and protection unit in 1998. "The statistics . . . '95.9 percent of children witnessed violence,' '79.6 percent lost a member of their family,' '31 percent witnessed rape.' UNICEF is trying to help the government to make a mental health policy in Rwanda in order to help all of the children."

One of the few Rwandan mental health professionals working on the problem of trauma counseling is Simon Gasibirege, a psychologist and professor at the University of Butare. Dr. Gasibirege directed a community mental health program created in 1995 that was a collaboration between his school and Louvain Catholic University in Belgium.

The program was working in four communes within the Butare prefecture several years after the genocide. It used an integrated community-based approach with interventions targeting not only children but the community at large. The staff, university teachers working for the center on a voluntary basis, trained over seven hundred authorities and volunteer community-based workers in community problem-solving and trauma-related issues.

"'Community mental health' with an emphasis on the community is atypical to the way a psychologist works with the individual," explained Dr. Gasibirege, who also had a pilot program with the support of Catholic Relief Services working with adolescents. "The psychologist works with the individual, and then the society has to deal with the person, but in Rwanda the society as a whole was destroyed. At our center, we cannot look only at specific traumas. Trauma is a multiplicity of losses.

"All Rwandans lost people, values, materials, goods, national unity," he continued. "Whether they were survivors of the genocide or returnees.

What is a community made of? Community? Solidarity? Management of conflicts? Following the genocide, all three were lost. Everyone belongs to a group, but these groups belong to a larger group. The focus should be on the act, not on who did what."

THE LAW

When the killings did stop, the legal system, undermanned and over-crowded, was ill-prepared to bring the accused to justice. Most weren't allowed to see lawyers or post any kind of bail for release. Among the 937,000 confirmed victims was a large percentage of the country's judiciary. Like many professions, the legal system suffered a major blow in 1994. Four years later, there were only fifty magistrates to hear cases in Rwanda, and the bar association was less than two years old. Two-thirds of Rwanda's judges either were killed or fled the country. Between 1997 and 1999, only 1,274 suspects had been tried. Foreign observers speculated it would take five hundred years to hear all the cases of genocide suspects.

After RPF forces stopped the genocide, the new Tutsi-led government was not forgiving. Along with five thousand other youths under the age of eighteen, François Minani was imprisoned for taking part in the genocide. "Some children killed more than five people, some children killed whole families, and some children killed other children who were in their class at school," noted Jean de Dieu Mucyo, who was the Minister of Justice when we first met but had become Prosecutor Generale by the last time I visited. "A person who would commit such a crime cannot just be put back into the community. The genocide was very well planned, and it was definitely in the plan for children to participate in it. However, there were some children who just followed the movement and decided to participate in the genocide on their own accord. In Rwanda killing is not only wrong; it is bad. It is taught as something that is bad in the Catholic Church. Because most of the population is Catholic it is clear that a lot of children knew that when they were killing it was bad. The children may not have known precisely what the written law was, but they had to have known that they were doing something serious. They knew that they were supposed to kill a specific race of people, and as a result they must have known that what they were doing would have real implications. In interviews the children were saying that they thought their group was the only group that should be in the world. The other impact of mass killing is that people are killed unintentionally, and many children killed people just because they looked like they were a particular race. The experiences of Rwanda cannot be compared to the experiences of another country. Rwanda has its own way of solving problems." Thousands of mostly Hutu suspects were rounded up and detained in prisons or *cacheaux* (jails). Years after the genocide, most prisoners hadn't been formally charged with a crime or allowed to see lawyers or post any kind of bail for release. Most disturbing was the integration of minors with adult prisoners, leading to widespread instances of physical abuse and rape.

"The problem is that Rwandan law says that children cannot be imprisoned under the age of fourteen," explained Luc Chauvin. "However, many children under the age of fourteen were imprisoned during the genocide. UNICEF tries to make sure that lawyers get fully briefed on what they need to do and that they know the situation they are coming into. This way they are able to make clear arguments and hopefully win cases. It is the first time that UNICEF has played such a big part because it is the first time that children have been so heavily involved in a genocide."

UNICEF worked with the government to build separate wings for juvenile prisoners as well as establish a "reeducation center" for those accused who were under the age of fourteen. Under Rwandan law, defendants under the age of fourteen years cannot be tried. Unlike South Africa, which chose to have a Truth and Reconciliation Commission document its apartheid-era atrocities and allow perpetrators to escape prosecution by admitting to the full scope of the crimes publicly, Rwandans are committed to prosecuting anyone who played even the slightest role. This marks the first time juveniles anywhere have faced charges for genocide—and François Minani is believed to have been the first juvenile in the world to be tried for such crimes.

François and I sat down for our first meeting at his parents' home in Gitarama a year and a half after his trial. A Rwandan human rights lawyer with LIPRODHOR (Rwandan League for the Promotion and Defense of Human Rights) arranged the visit. It had rained nonstop the day we trudged down the slick, muddy path up which François had led his nephews to their deaths. A hunched, thin woman with a scarf wrapping her head came out of the hut to greet us. A small child peered at us from behind a wooden pen for chickens.

Our escort, the lawyer, introduced everyone in the group, and then François came out. Wearing a slightly lopsided afro, black floral print shirt, and jeans, he wasn't who I expected. He was medium height, thinly built, and handsome in a rough way. Chairs were brought outside, and he and I sat facing each other. To my disbelief and confusion, we were going to talk outside in full view of his family and neighbors, who were crowded around us on rocks, the ground, and the hill. The lawyer was going to translate from Kinyarwanda into French for me.

Although I was directly across from him, François wouldn't look at me. He kept his eyes turned toward the translator or at a clump of rocks and brush over the man's shoulder.

"I was imprisoned because the militia took me and told me to commit the genocide," François began, speaking very low. I looked around to gauge the reaction of the people around us, but everyone seemed more curious with our presence there than with what François had to say. "I lived here with my parents," he continued. "A group arrived here and took me to a camp away from here. They were men, and they took me by force. They wanted to bury me. When I saw they were going to kill me, I did what they showed me to do."

Five months later, in October 1994, he was taken by RPF soldiers to prison. It was three years before François would be brought to trial. In the interim, he lived in the Gitarama Central Prison not far from his home. "I was very afraid," he told me. "The counsel of the community asked me to come to the center of town. When I got there, I found lots of soldiers all around. The judicial police interrogated me; then I went to prison." François confessed to his crimes and even wrote a letter of apology, asking forgiveness from the community and his family. The two people whom he'd passed en route to the pit for the Tutsi victims verified his version of the story. His parents gave statements. There, the process stopped.

The first week inside a cell with thousands of other suspects was rough on François. He had nothing to eat or drink and nowhere to sleep regularly. Sometimes he could scrounge up a sandwich to last a week but nothing on a steady basis. His reliance on the power of prayer got him through the ordeal.

When he faced the Gitarama Court of First Instance on September 23, 1997, François Minani was classified in the second category of genocide suspects: those who killed or committed violent acts but were not planners. There were no witnesses called by the prosecution, as all necessary statements had been taken three years before. Besides, he'd confessed, which could have meant a twelve-year sentence for him.

Since he'd been forced to kill his nephews and had already spent three years in prison, he was found guilty of genocide, fined five thousand

Rwandan francs, and sentenced to five years in prison. He never served the remaining two years but returned to what was left of his family.

François went home a scarred, empty man. After three years in the Gitarama Central Prison, he received no counseling support from the government following his release, nor was there any type of coordination with his home community. When he returned, most of the residents accepted him, but there were a few survivors who tried to have him sent back to prison. "They had their reasons," he said somberly. An elder brother was also sent to prison, but he was innocent of genocidal charges and was released a short while later.

No child under the age of eighteen at the time of the killings was accused of organizing genocidal acts, but many were charged with murder or held indefinitely and not charged at all. Other genocide-related crimes included rape, property damage, and theft. Those youth held without being charged were placed with imprisoned relatives, for their own protection against acts of vengeance. According to Article 77 of the Rwandan Penal Code, the harshest sentence a youth fourteen to eighteen years old could receive was twenty years' imprisonment.

The Ministry of Justice was able to reorganize the juvenile justice system in 1996. With the assistance of UNICEF and Avocats Sans Frontières (Lawyers without Borders), a task force of forty investigators was created to deal with the overwhelming caseload. The two groups supported special investigators and prosecutors responsible for the cases of minors. Many Rwandan defense lawyers wouldn't take on clients accused of genocidal crimes for fear of reprisals by victims' families. Fewer than one hundred detained minors in the country had their case files sent to specialized chambers for youth. More staggering was the fact that at least 30 percent of all imprisoned children had no case files, making it nearly impossible for them to move through the system.

"The changes that have occurred with regard to the prisons have not been in security," noted Minister of Justice Mucyo. "The guards have remained the same, but the changes have come in the administration. So the changes have not really affected the children that much. However, recently a new rule was made that said that all children must go through the Ministry of Justice before they go to a prison. Therefore there is now a delay in the process. The system has not changed very much, but there are more people in the jails, and more cases in courts. As a result special genocide panels have been formed in order to produce more cases having to do with the genocide. The courts in the Ministry of Justice are divided. Some courts only deal with cases that involve the genocide, and some courts deal with cases that involve every crime." With UNICEF's help, the Ministry of Justice constructed wings for minors in five of the country's ten prisons. It was an unusual role, but the agency wanted to protect the youth from the sexual abuse they faced when thrown in jail with adults.

INSIDE THE GIKONDO-KIGALI PRISON

At the time of my first of two visits to Gikondo-Kigali Prison in the fall of 1998, there were 869 juveniles incarcerated, the highest number in Rwanda. High metal doors surrounded the compound. Gikondo was the largest of three facilities in Kigali with adults and youths. The juvenile wing opened in December 1996. Previously housed with adult offenders, boys had been exploited by older prisoners. Many children had a father, brothers, and cousins on the neighboring adult side. A winding dirt road marked with holes and jagged ridges led to the redbrick prison compound, which was tucked away in one of the city's poorest neighborhoods. A white sign staked alongside the road announced simply "Prison." Two soldiers greeted us outside the gate's fortress-like metal doors. It used to be an open-air market owned by a *genocidaire*, local French for someone who committed a genocidal crime.

Like every other penal institution in Rwanda, the inmates policed themselves; there were no guards inside. The director and his staff padlocked each wing from the outside. Everyone wore a pink uniform, though they were supposedly for adults only. The prisoners elected a *capitaine generale* who oversaw day-to-day operations. Under him were yellow-bereted "trustees"—forty-two of them—who carried long wooden sticks to intimidate or beat fellow prisoners who got out of line. It was a true-life version of *Lord of the Flies*.

Inside the children's area was a large dirt courtyard and adjoining hangar-like dormitory. The common area resembled a little city. To the right was the kitchen, where meals were prepared twice a day. To the left were the prison's amenities, a row of twenty-four showers and twelve toilets for the entire inmate population. A thick stench of sweat and human waste hung in the air.

The Gikondo Prison's most disturbing aspect was its sleeping quarters. The dark, cavernous space burst with row upon row of bunk beds, two bodies to a bed. Inmate-guards and older inmates copped the top bunks. Burlap sacks of personal belongings, calendars, old pinups from American magazines, and music posters lined the walls.

Ndagizarana Eric, age nineteen, was the youth *capitaine generale*. A slightly built teenager wearing white high-top sneakers and a worn baseball cap pulled down over his eyes, Eric had been at Gikondo for three years when we met. He told me he'd gotten his position soon after arriving. "I was greatly respected and motivated to succeed," he said with a cryptic smile.

"The major concern here is access to justice," explained Eric, who like many others claimed not to have a case file or to have seen a lawyer. Three people in the prison had been tried. One youth received a five-year sentence, and two adults were sentenced to death.

I asked Eric what he'd done to end up in Gikondo.

Raising his head slowly, he replied, "Genocide."

The second time I visited the facility, an unsettling discovery was awaiting among the imprisoned youths. A handful of boys were cutting firewood in a far corner. Another section was occupied by a group of Christian inmates singing gospel songs in French. Most detainees milled around in the middle, playing soccer and chatting. An official accompanying us made the troubling discovery of a twelve-year-old inmate named Mbonizina Boniface. Because of his age, he shouldn't have been there. He would have been seven years old at the time of the genocide. Boniface wore a vacant expression and was generally unresponsive to questions.

The older inmates, who apparently had been taking care of him since he got there, said he could remember very little about his family or home.

"We need to make a distinction between the management of the prison and the prosecution," explained Rukerikibaye John, then-deputy director at Gikondo. "We are not responsible for bringing these kids here. That is up to the prosecutors."

When questioned about the presence of underage inmates in Rwanda's prison system, Minister of Justice Mucyo was defensive. "People have to be very careful because it is often difficult to determine the age of the child who has committed the crime," he noted. "Once the age is calculated, however, the child is dealt with properly. A big problem is that some people do not know about the age law, and some people will throw children in jail without paying any attention to their ages. People are being released more often, but before they are released, a full investigation must be done. It is possible that people are in prison in one area, but the crime they committed was in another area; therefore it takes a long time to do these investigations."

Emmanueal Hitayezu was a nineteen-year-old youth I met who'd been at Gikondo for four years. He claimed to have never seen a lawyer since being locked up. His crew voiced the same complaint. No one would talk about the war directly. One short teenager wearing a dark tank top and shorts could only remember that he had worked as a craftsperson before the war.

"I've been accused of genocide," was all he would say as explanation for being locked up. "My father fell ill during the war and died, but my mother comes to visit and brings me food. Before coming here, I was at Kigali Central Prison. It was a frightening place. The kids never had any food, and older prisoners took advantage. It's much better here. The kids are not my family, but they have been my friends."

REEDUCATION

For those juveniles sent to regular prisons or deemed underage at the time of the genocide, more hope could be found at the Gitagata Reeducation Center, a former reform school an hour's drive southeast of Kigali. It had housed juvenile delinquents since 1975. Gitagata reopened in June 1995 with the help of UNICEF, after having been destroyed in the war.

"The reeducation center has provided a good place for the children to be instead of jail," noted Chauvin. "The program operates by saying that these children were imprisoned under the age of fourteen and therefore do not belong in prison. Another program that UNICEF operates deals with children who are arrested over the age of fourteen and therefore can be held criminally responsible. For those children, we see that they are given lawyers and the right to a fair trial. In this way, the Rwandan law can be applied fairly."

For five years, hundreds of Rwandans who were too young to be held legally responsible for their actions were sent to the Gitagata Reeducation Center. In 2002, it switched its focus to handling street kids sent by the national police. Although he was considered a juvenile at the time of the genocide, François was too old for Gitagata and spent three years in prison. Defendants fourteen to eighteen years of age can be tried for criminal actions in Rwanda but never receive the death penalty and tend to get comparatively light sentences. From 1994 to 2002, juvenile justice in Rwanda focused on dealing with youth who had somehow participated in the genocide, but in subsequent years the priority shifted to those committing everyday crimes.

When I visited Gitagata, 327 youth between ten and nineteen years old were living there. The youngest person ever sent to Gitagata was an eight-year-old boy who'd thrown a grenade into a crowd of children. In the four years since its reopening, only two boys had run away—one went home to his family, and the other later returned to the center. There were also a few youths there for crimes like stealing and rape, but they didn't stay long.

"They must at least go through a reeducation center," said Minister Mucyo. "The children who are in prison now are just there temporarily. Do you think a child that killed five other children should be put back in the community, or should they be put in a specific place for reeducation? One reeducation center is sufficient because that one center has been successful in terms of reuniting children with their families. There are many people in the prisons, and the truth is that there should be more people."

After the center reopened following the end of the genocide, initial reports suggested older prisoners had sexually abused younger ones there, too. The problem was handled when the youths organized a security staff among themselves.

"When children arrive to the reeducational center, they are identified and registered," explained Casimir Karasira, the bearded, soft-spoken director of Gitagata. A seminary professor, he'd been trained as a trauma advisor at the National Trauma Center. "Then the rehabilitation process begins immediately. Every afternoon, the children are taken into small sessions to discuss the conflict and differences between good and bad."

29

Prior to daily counseling, the boys attended school or learned vocational skills such as carpentry, tailoring, or farming. The counselors broke them up into small groups and assigned them caregivers who tracked each individual's progress. At the start of incarceration, every child received a card on which progress was monitored. Before they could be sent home to their families, local agencies and the center's staff prepared the community in advance. An apology by the child and a formal request for forgiveness from the community were mandatory. In four years' time, 187 children were returned to their families and communities. The *enadreur*, a caseworker, proposed the names of those who seemed most ready and had displayed the most significant changes in behavior and outlook.

Family reintegration from Gitagata required a lot of preparation. First, there was the establishment of a reintegration commission followed by a briefing of the local "bourgemeister," or mayor of the commune. A communal meeting was called to explain to residents about the law regarding children who committed crimes under the age of fourteen. The population was also reminded that these children were encouraged and pushed by adults; then the community members were asked to accept the youngster back into their fold. One or two meetings might have been necessary before the youth was asked to apologize publicly. He was also encouraged to denounce the person or persons who incited him to kill.

The first few years of Gitagata's handling of youth *genocidaires* were not always rosy. Over a dozen youths were refused by their communities or family members. In one case a parent said that the child in question was difficult even before the genocide. Eventually the boy went to live with an aunt. The real age of the others was a main reason for refusal by their home communities. If community members suspected or knew that the youth were older than they admitted, the community would not accept them back. It was thought that many at the center had lied about their ages in order to avoid the harsher conditions of a regular prison, but without birth certificates or corroborating documents, center administrators were forced to accept the stated ages.

The successes were credited to the trust developed between the boys and their counselors, observers told me. "To their counselors, the kids will share everything," remarked a UNICEF staffer, "but to those of us on the outside, nothing."

The *capitaine generale* at Gitagata was an eighteen-year-old in a white T-shirt, flip-flops, and shorts. His name was Jerome, and he'd overseen security for three of his four years at the center. Sitting on the steps leading to the main building, he expressed profound frustration with being in any kind of detention. He was anxious to get home.

"I was originally in Kigali Central Prison, but because of my age they moved me here," he said. "They blamed me, with a group of others, for hunting down some people who were in hiding and killing them. I was associated with my older brother who was missing at the time. I committed no crime.

"I've been here for so long because there is a long waiting list for people ready to leave," he continued. "Soon, it should be my turn to go home. I hope to take up a trade and be with my family again."

RELEASE

In October 1998, the Rwandan Ministry of Justice began releasing prisoners. At that time, ten thousand people without case files were let go, and in the years since, thousands more have been released without trial. By spring of 2004, approximately twenty thousand prisoners were taken from prisons across Rwanda to so-called solidarity camps operated by the Ministry of Unity and Reconciliation. The period of stay at these centers could last between one and three months, and individuals were essentially indoctrinated with Rwandan history, the necessity of coexistence, the moral implications of the genocide, and vocational training. Also, former soldiers of the war in the Democratic Republic of Congo were sent to solidarity camps before being allowed to return home.

A further response to the overwhelming demands on a skeletal justice system in the process of repair was the creation of *gaccaca*, a community-level response to the genocide whereby everyday citizens investigated, prosecuted, and punished offenders with whom they had worked and lived. Defendants received half the sentence they would in a national court but were also required to do some form of public service as part of their punishment.

Once it was fully activated throughout the whole country, organizers expected that six times the sixty thousand people already tried in national courts for genocide would be charged. Because of the number of years many accused had already been held without due process of law, they were often released fairly quickly into their home communities through *gaccaca*. A plea-bargaining process allowed individuals to confess to their crimes in exchange for light sentences.

"As time moves on, people become more receptive to the releases," noted Aloys Habimana, program director of LIPRODHOR, which was forced to shut down by the government in the spring of 2004. "The biggest issue with *gaccaca* is the unwillingness of people to talk. Witnesses don't want to bring shame on themselves, especially if they've been raped or sexually assaulted. There's also the risk of retribution for testifying against a defendant."

A former protection officer with UNICEF and the wife of Kigali's mayor, Domitille Mukantaganzwa was executive secretary of the National Service of Gaccaca Jurisdictions. An elegant woman with a bob haircut and an office facing the rear of the National Stadium, Mukantaganzwa was much more optimistic about the potential of the *gaccaca* process for justice and national healing. "The population directs *gaccaca*," she explained with a smile. "Sometimes it is very difficult to get to the truth. In five years we will know where we are in the process. With the strategy we are using, the process of *gaccaca* and trying all the genocide defendants can be finished if we have the right resources."

The fact that a painful search for truth and justice for genocide victims and survivors would take many more years was obvious during the commemoration period marking its tenth anniversary, officially known as "Rwanda 10." Just as the genocide in Rwanda lasted one hundred days, so did the observance of it in 2004. United Nations Secretary-General Kofi Annan spoke about the genocide at the New York headquarters in the days before ceremonies began in Rwanda. Annan had been in charge of the organization's peacekeeping under then Secretary-General Boutros Boutros-Ghali. "I realized after the genocide that there was more that I could and should have done to sound the alarm and rally support," he admitted. For Rwandans and many Africans, a great blame rests with Annan for not allowing peacekeepers to intervene.

Following a memorial event in the town of Gisozi on April 8 to open a new genocide center, an hour-long ceremony was held at the National Stadium with performances by the Ballet National du Rwanda, the National Army band, and scores of invited artists from around the African continent. In prior years services included a series of speeches, but that time organizers wanted to have Rwandan children speak as the voices of victims and survivors, to convey the legacy. The tone was decidedly different, almost celebratory.

"We commemorate the dead because we have loved them, and want to remember them," explained François Girambe, chairman of a national survivors' group called Ibuka, at a press conference for Rwanda 10. "Humankind can never have peace if it has not accomplished its task of learning. We commemorate to fight the possibility of forgetting the geno-cide and the denials that it ever took place. Understanding is a weapon against forgetting."

In anticipation of the tenth anniversary, dozens of communities across Rwanda started searching for missing loved ones and neighbors in order to rebury them properly. It was such a search that I observed in Kibuye at the hospital and hillside. Nearly all the victims killed were interred in mass graves. The British-based organization Aegis Trust collaborated with the government to identify and collect photographs of all the geno-cide's victims, as well as build a handful of memorial sites throughout the country for educational purposes. Eighty genocide survivors working with Aegis went from house to house to collect the names and photo-graphs of the victims.

"The genocide was the biggest foreign affairs failure in the last de-cade," noted James Smith, a cofounder of Aegis Trust with his brother Stephen and the husband of a genocide survivor. He also pointed out the appearance of a continuing lack of interest in Rwanda by the absence of Western leaders during the national commemoration. Belgium's prime minister was the only Western head of state to attend. "It makes one pes-simistic about what would happen if another genocide occurred."

The American delegation was led not by President George W. Bush or Secretary of State Colin Powell, but Pierre-Richard Prosper, Ambassador-at-Large for War Crimes Issues. The forty-year-old Haitian-American was the first prosecutor for the International Criminal Tribunal for Rwanda (ICTR) in Arusha, Tanzania. A former U.S. district attorney, Prosper is still affected by the three years he spent trying architects of the genocide.

"Being here after ten years, what it really does is provide an opportu-nity to reflect, not just on the genocide but to look back over the last ten years and realize we could have done more," he admitted, sitting in the lobby of Kigali's Intercontinental Hotel after a day of photo-ops and site visits. "The experience of being an ICTR prosecutor was an important one because it showed one the do's and don'ts in a post-conflict setting. Now that I'm sitting in a policy seat, it puts situations like Iraq, Sierra Leone, and the Balkans in better perspective. Part of the problem is that what happened here is incomprehensible. Rather than taking the time, it's easier to pause, shake your head, and move on. In America, we like to understand things very quickly. Going back to L.A. after three years, I faced two responses to my time here. Either a person wouldn't leave me alone and bothered me all night about the details, which was rare. Or, they would say, 'Wow! That sounds amazing.' Then we'd start talking about the Los Angeles Dodgers."

Not until the fall of 1994 did Pierre-Richard Prosper fully understand what had happened in Rwanda. A first-generation Haitian-American, the bright, handsome lawyer was on a political fast track. He had spent five years as a deputy district attorney in his native Los Angeles and gone on to serve as an assistant U.S. attorney for the Central District of California in Los Angeles. Attending a social function, he overheard someone talking about the genocide and the legal and other problems Rwanda faced in the aftermath. His curiosity piqued, Prosper started asking questions and doing research. Several months later, he was approached through State Department channels about becoming lead prosecutor at the ICTR. Running parallel to the national trials and court system in Rwanda, the ICTR was created through the United Nations to try the leaders and planners of the Rwandan genocide. The court had several groundbreaking proceedings, including the first prosecution of a woman, Pauline Nyirmasuhuko, Rwanda's minister of family and women's development, for genocide and crimes against humanity.

From a third-floor cubicle in the office space of an Arusha shopping center, Prosper led an international team of lawyers that prosecuted Jean-Paul

Akayesu, a provincial mayor who had caused the deaths and mass rapes of hundreds of his constituents. Prosper worked in Tanzania and Rwanda for three years before returning to the United States in 1998.

In 2001, Prosper was selected as United States ambassador-at-large for war crimes issues. He was responsible for overseeing treatment, behavior, and adjudication of war criminals at the U.S. military base at Guantanamo Bay in Cuba, as well as investigating human rights abuses in places such as the Sudan, where the Arab government was supporting a campaign of genocide against Christians.

"In regard to Rwanda," he observed, "we should have engaged immediately at the first warning sign. Even if neighboring states hadn't said something, we could have done something sooner. You can't look away and hope the problem goes away."

FRANÇOIS

Ten years after the death of his sister and her children and two years after marrying and fathering a son, François Minani wished he'd made a different choice. "Then, I was a very young boy and when you're a boy, sometimes you don't know what to do, what to choose," he told me, sitting in front of the same ragged hut where we'd spoken five years before. Physically he hadn't changed much. His hair was shorter, and he had a thin moustache, but his wiry build and evasive gaze remained the same. He was dressed in a black and white striped shirt, grey slacks, and black boots with white laces and no socks. Again, a crowd of milling family members, friends, and curious children from the village were scattered around the dirt yard and slope around us.

He was back home in Gitarama, with its muddy roads and brick homes with roofs of corrugated steel. Driving to meet him, I was reminded of fields of sorghum and poverty. Things hadn't gone well for François since we'd met. His parents died, and after two years of working in Kigali as a domestic, he returned home. Another sister and her children were living there, but he didn't get along with her. They argued mostly about money, in particular the lack of it.

In fact, he'd been living in Taba but had to flee with his wife, Brigitte, and their young son. A number of people in the community had accused him of stealing, and he wasn't that far from being locked up. He'd stolen simple items such as an ax and a chicken, but in a poor community that was serious. "There have not been so many changes in five years," he said. "Problems in my life are many because of a lack of resources and job. It is not easy, this life."

Brigitte, twenty-seven, was originally from Gikondo. He met her in Kigali, where they worked in the same compound. That position actually followed one at the home of a lawyer for LIPRODHOR. Laid off, he returned to Gitarama in March 2002.

In order to make ends meet, François worked cultivating beans, sweet potatoes, and cassava. "It was very difficult to come home, because at least in Kigali I could get work," he lamented. "The space here is really too small to farm the land. I'm not very hopeful about the future."

A typical day for him was drowning in monotony. Waking up in the mornings, he would go into the fields with a hoe. After an hour's break, François would go into the main town in the afternoon to look for work. In the evenings he would return to bathe and sleep. Before moving to Kigali, he would always go for a late walk, but he stopped doing so when he returned.

Despite the local and international attention given to the tenth commemoration of the genocide, François had no plans to do anything special. "Maybe I'll be with my family and others in the community to reflect on the victims," he suggested. "In the past, I've never had any problems, and I hope there won't be any this year.

"I have forgiven myself for what happened in the genocide, for what I did," he continued. "Sometimes when I think about it, I feel guilty, but at other times I don't. Always I ask myself, 'Why did the genocide happen?' I used to have nightmares, but now they have stopped."

Surprisingly, he hadn't told his wife why he was in prison, although I suspected our reunion would raise the issue. "She's never asked. But my son, Frank Mucyo, I think I will tell him what happened. If I have a chance to still be alive when he's an adult, I have to tell him what happened. Things might get worse at any time, and you never know if you'll be alive to see your children become adults."

NOTES

1. Binaifer Nowrojee, *Shattered Lives: Sexual Violence during the Rwandan Genocide and Its Aftermath* (New York: Human Rights Watch, 1996), 2.

2

"Sometimes I Feel Like Killing":
Violent Childhoods in Colombia

SMOKE FROM MORTARS and grenade explosions hung thickly in the midnight air the first time he fought in combat, but he barely noticed. Automatic fire from M60 machine guns provided a symphony of chaos. "I saw a lot of my comrades killed or wounded," recalled Luís, who fired blindly into the ensuing chaos. "After you've been in battle, your blood gets warm," he explained to me, "and you don't feel the cold."

Fear is another matter. Desertion meant certain death at the hands of his guerilla commanders. For courage, he took off the tip of a bullet and ate the lead powder inside. It didn't work.

He and several hundred members of the FARC—Fuerzas Armadas Revolucionarias De Colombia, or the Revolutionary Armed Forces of Colombia, one of the most powerful guerilla groups in Latin America—

The names of all children mentioned in Chapter 2 have been changed to protect their identities.

had been ordered by commanders to lay siege on a rural police station in central Colombia. The guerillas faced a defiant police squad and army reinforcements. Luís began shooting with an AK–47. Aside from eight months of jungle boot camp, he had never been to school. The young soldier was proficient with an AK–47 but had never even held a pencil.

About thirty insurgents would rotate to the front of the assault line every half hour, collecting discarded guns and wounded before retreating. "I was afraid I'd be killed," he admitted in a quiet, calm voice, eyes focused downward, while sitting at a chipped wooden table with his hands folded in front of him. I was sitting with him in the staff conference room of a rehabilitation center about an hour outside Bogotá, the capital. It was five years after the incident he described to me. Given the intensity of his story, I hadn't expected him to talk about it as easily as he did. Less than fifteen minutes after meeting me, he took me on a journey of his painful memories. We spoke through a translator, and three staff workers at the center sat in the room with us, but we might as well have been alone sharing stories. His knuckles were tattooed with the initials E, L, N, and F, representing former girlfriends. The frail-looking youth was scrawny and so shy that he couldn't hold eye contact with me for long. In the fleeting moments when I could catch his eyes, the deep sadness behind them was painfully obvious.

"Your training reminds you that you either die or survive," he continued. "That's the law of the jungle. You never know if your shots hit someone because there are thirty of you firing in one direction, and thirty firing back. I thought, 'I should find another way of living, of moving forward into the fight. One has to be brave to fight an enemy.'"

Twenty-four hours after the initial assault, the rebels took the station along with twenty-eight police officers as prisoners. The next time Luís fought, he wasn't scared anymore.

Luís was twelve years old.

LA VIOLENCIA

Contrary to what Americans and perhaps many others in the world believe, the conflict in Colombia is not solely about drugs, but also about class, economics, and power. Cocaine is merely the ugly means for perpetuating a seemingly unwinnable war. Over generations, children have been the main casualties, both as the victims of violence and as the perpetrators of it.

The longer that conflicts—international or national—continue, the more likely that children will be exploited as soldiers. The more adult males who are wounded, killed, or captured, the more youngsters will become the inevitable recruiting pool. And whenever children are used to fight, all youth are jeopardized. Between six thousand and fourteen thousand Colombians under the age of eighteen are members of armed groups. Additionally, two million civilians have been displaced from their homes, and three million children have no access to educational opportunities. In 2004, the United Nations described the situation in Colombia as the largest human rights crisis in the Western Hemisphere.

Colombia has been at war since it gained independence from Spain in 1810, nearly two hundred years ago, and for about sixty years, it has endured "La Violencia." This period of strife began after the 1948 assassination of Jorge Eliecer Gaitan, a Liberal Party presidential candidate. Several hundred thousand Colombians died in the fighting that immediately followed Gaitan's death. Despite a brokered political agreement, social inequities were not fully addressed, and in 1964, sixteen years after the start of La Violencia, fighting resumed, as abandoned communist insurgents created FARC. A year later, the ELN (Ejercito Nacional de Liberacion or National Liberation Army) was formed as an alternative leftist revolutionary organization, but like the FARC it fought against wealthy landowners and a conservative government.[1] The FARC claims to be fighting on behalf of the common people's economic and political rights

41

but has no qualms about using terror, kidnapping, and drug trafficking to succeed. Of the two, it is considerably larger and better known internationally than the ELN.

As a defense against the leftists, businessmen, property owners, and sympathetic army commanders created the AUC (Autodefensas Unidas del Sur del Casanare, or United Self-Defense Forces of Colombia), a right-wing coalition of paramilitary groups allied with the state. In the current military dynamic, government forces are fighting both the ELN and the FARC, with the unofficial support of the paramilitary AUC. All three non-governmental forces are on the U.S. State Department list of terrorists, though the Colombian government has moved to disarm and quell the activities of paramilitaries, most often blamed for abuses and civilian massacres.

The majority of the child soldiers in Colombia, like Luís, are members of the FARC, and a much smaller fraction serve in the ELN. Through its involvement in drug trafficking to the international community, the FARC has become one of the wealthiest guerilla groups in the world, and its ranks in the last decade are thought to be between fifteen thousand and twenty thousand, a significant percentage of them children.

Boys and girls as young as eight years old are recruited by the FARC, AUC, and the ELN, often forcibly. These kids face harsh punishment, including death, if they try to return to civilian life. Not just used as fighters, child soldiers in Colombia spy, carry messages, guard kidnap victims, and place bombs.

Until February 21, 2002, FARC controlled Farclandia, a demilitarized zone the size of Switzerland. The government of then president Ernesto Samper had withdrawn its military forces from the region for the purpose of jump-starting peace talks. That month, however, Samper suspended talks because of alleged FARC violations, and negotiations with the ELN fell apart in June of the same year.

Though overshadowed by high-profile fighting in places such as Iraq and Afghanistan, the American military has maintained a significant presence and role in Colombia for a number of years. In the fall of 2002, the U.S. Congress approved a request from the Bush administration to allow American military aid, previously targeted against the drug trade, to be used against insurgents, namely the FARC and ELN. Both the Colombian and American governments insist that fighting drugs is a major component of dealing with the anti-government guerillas as well as the pro-government, right-wing paramilitaries. That was the initial reasoning behind "Plan Colombia," a $1.3 billion assistance package pushed by President Bill Clinton to combat the growth and production of cocaine in the mid to late '90s. Starting in the late 70s and going into the 1980s, illegal drugs became a factor in Colombia's civil war. In the decades since, the conflict itself has become fueled in large part by the drug trafficking of the FARC and the AUC. Colombia now supplies 90 percent of the cocaine in the United States.

Beatriz Linares, with the Office of the People's Advocates, noted some important points about children and the Colombian war. "The research has uncovered that deep social conflicts are at the root of children's direct participation in the conflict," wrote Linares. "Social exclusion, mistreatment, lack of educational opportunities, and lack of jobs in rural and marginal areas drive children to abandon their homes and seek a better life with the guerillas. Nearly 83 percent of children who enlist in the illegal armed groups do so voluntarily. The war necessarily generates a leaning towards a culture of violence, particularly among children who have only known violence."[2]

Only in the last decade have the civilian population and the government taken real notice of the problem. On November 11, 2000, the Fifth Brigade of the Colombian army engaged the "Arturo Ruiz" Column of the FARC in what is referred to as Operacion Berlin. Government soldiers faced 380 FARC fighters in Surata, a town in the state of Santander, in a bloodbath. More than half the guerillas were killed, including twenty children. Nine of those slain kids were girls whose autopsied bodies showed they'd suffered sexual abuse and had intrauterine devices (IUDs) implanted. The Colombian army primarily uses aerial bombardments in its offensives against guerillas and often doesn't know if children or adults are being wounded and killed.

Of the seventy-seven FARC combatants taken alive, thirty-two were under the age of eighteen years. It was a shock to the nation and its view of the conflict up to that point. Those children who were captured accused the army of physical and verbal abuse, and testified to being threatened with burning and beatings for not providing information about the guerillas.

When President Alvaro Uribe decided in the fall of 2004 that the fighting between guerillas and government forces did not constitute war but was instead a struggle against terrorism, it threatens to worsen the lives of Colombian children: international relief organizations such as the Red Cross and the United Nations High Commissioner for Refugees do not have a mandate to work in a country that is besieged by a "terrorist" struggle rather than conflict. The Colombian Institute of Forensic Medicine found that an estimated five Colombian children are murdered every day, and 40 percent of slain guerillas—FARC and ELN—are under the age of eighteen.

International and domestic organizations in Colombia face a tough challenge in finding the antidotes to decades of violence against Colombia's children. One dreary, overcast morning in Bogotá shortly after my arrival in Colombia, I spent several hours with Manuel Manrique Castro, then head of the UNICEF mission. A Peruvian children's rights advocate, Castro had been in the country for a year. As we sat in his twelfth-floor office overlooking the downtown business district, he pointed out to me why the level of pervasive, everyday violence in Colombian society is unlike any other. "The Colombian army must deal not only with two formidable guerilla groups in the FARC and ELN, but under recent U.S. pressure must rein in the paramilitaries of the AUC," he noted. "Thirty-four kidnappings happen daily somewhere in Colombia, and the murder rate is the highest in the world, military and non-military.

"Second, there is of course the drug factor," he added. "Unlike wars in South Asia or even some places in Africa, the non-governmental combatants are mostly self-sustaining and survive without outside assistance."

Land mines are also an issue, according to Castro. Almost five hundred municipalities have been mined. The guerillas are known to surround the area with onions and other means of throwing off the scent of search dogs. "Children are inevitably the ones who step on them," he observed. No humanitarian mine-clearance programs are in place in Colombia.

UNICEF's most visible accomplishment in assisting war-affected children in Colombia has been in the area of peace-building and advocacy. The Nobel Prize–nominated Children's Movement for Peace grew out of a 1996 workshop sponsored by UNICEF to educate children and women's groups about the Convention on the Rights of the Child (CRC). Adopted by the United Nations General Assembly in late 1989, the CRC identifies and promises the protection of the basic rights of children throughout the world and is the most ratified treaty in modern history. Only two countries have failed to ratify it: the failed state of Somalia and the United States. Nearly a decade later, one hundred thousand youths throughout Colombia are working with the Children's Movement for Peace to lobby for reconciliation and peace in their communities.

"BOOM!"

The use of child soldiers is not a new phenomenon, but they are more noticeable now because of the increased availability of automatic weapons.

An M16 or AK–47 assault rifle is much easier for a child to disassemble, clean, and load than a bolt-action weapon or heavy carbine. The same goes for grenade tubes and shoulder-fired rocket launchers.

No one can know how many weapons are being used in Colombia, but we do know which ones: the Galil (an Israeli automatic rifle), the Kalashnikov, .9mm pistols, M4 carbines, M14s, M16s, fragmentation grenades, AR–15s, which can penetrate concrete, and Claymore mines. It's no wonder four thousand Colombian children under eighteen die annually, primarily from war-related causes and disease, according to UNICEF.[3]

While the Colombian military receives its weapons legitimately through direct purchases or military aid, the aligned paramilitary groups arm themselves through narcotics dealing and support from the army. The FARC and ELN, of course, acquire weapons illegally through drugs and kidnapping, smuggling them in through border countries such as Venezuela and Ecuador. According to the Small Arms Survey of 2002, AK–47s in Colombia go for the lowest prices in the world for used weapons, $800 each. A result is a homicide count of about twenty thousand a year.

Not too long ago, it was Duilio's job to lay down mines. Like Luís, he was no longer fighting when we met, but instead working to rebuild his former life. Originally from Cesar province near the coast of the Atlantic Ocean, he joined the ELN at age thirteen for economic and personal motivations, becoming a mine expert. His unit operated in San Pablo, a heavily contested area in northern Colombia.

A heavy rain had just ended in the city of Cali, where Duilio was then living, as he related his story to me. He, five other boys, and two adults shared an apartment, one of many on a street lined with brick houses of various colors with stucco roofs. Duilio at first looked like a typical seventeen-year-old, dressed in boots, jeans, and a knit shirt—except he was missing his right eye and most of his left hand.

We sat in the front room of the apartment on adjacent sofas that faced a window looking onto the street one floor below. "I was in school until I was ten years old and then left to work selling fruit," he said, somberly. "After I left to join the ELN, the first three months were the regular training you get. Then, there were six more months dealing with explosives during which time I was in combat as well. There were something like twenty or thirty people my age in the column, but for explosives I was the youngest."

A mine can explode in one of three ways: if someone steps on it, if someone turns it over, or if someone attaches a cable and detonates it from a distance. "You're walking along and then, 'Boom!'" explained Duilio.

On the morning of April 6, 2001, when Duilio was fifteen, he was sent on a mission with two other young comrades to lay down a minefield in an area where the AUC normally traveled, in the Bolivar province. Duilio was putting his fiftieth mine into the ground when he made his first and last mistake.

"Once you know how to do something sometimes, you don't always do it as carefully as you might," he observed, wistfully. "Too much confidence."

One of his friends made a joke, and Duilio turned around to listen. When he went back to the job, he knocked the mine over, and it exploded in his face.

"I just felt like, 'Oops!' It felt like there was an ant farm inside of me. I told my friends, 'If I die, please set me down on the side of the highway and send my body to where my parents will know what happened.'"

Duilio was sent to a center in Bucaramanga, where he was given prostheses for his eye and hand and treated for brain trauma. But his ordeal was not over.

He was transferred to a hospital for mentally retarded people, only to have paramilitary soldiers take him away to the headquarters of the infamous

AUC commander Carlos Castano. For the next eight days Duilio was interrogated about what he knew of the ELN's operations, where he'd laid down mines, and what training he'd received. When Castano finally made an appearance, Duilio knew him immediately from television reports.

"I was between a sword and a wall at that point," noted Duilio. "If [the AUC was] going to kill me, they could kill me with pleasure. I said to Castano, 'Just shoot me right now in the head, but don't torture me.'"

Startled by the young boy's courage, the hardened soldier replied, "Why are you telling me that? I'm not going to kill you!"

The paramilitary wanted to bring Duilio over to their side and send him on a mission to locate and deactivate mines. They even offered him a salary of five hundred thousand pesos, or approximately $500.

The brain damage he endured from the explosion was severe, though, affecting his short-term memory and ability to do basic things. After having been on the opposing side of the battlefield and suffering from severely debilitating injuries, he declined their offer. Consequently, he was turned over to the government.

When we spoke in the fall of 2002, it had been a year since Duilio recovered his memory. Returning to his home village, where his former comrades could accuse him of collaboration with the government, was out of the question. He had moved to Cali a month before, after a period of rehabilitation, and planned on studying auto mechanics and eventually attending college. Duilio also crocheted to improve the dexterity in his deformed hand. (Stress in my own life would lead me to take up knitting myself a short time later, a development I wish I could have shared with this impressive young man.)

"You imagine that the thing is still there," he had told me, looking down at his deformed hand. "I just have the attitude that you give yourself strength. I don't know why I'm like that, but that thinking has been good for me. I want to be trained in something so I can help my family."

In a country like Colombia, where young people have been going to war too early, for far too long, resilience may be the one true victory.

MAJOR CASTILLO

Shortly after arriving in Colombia, the first place I visited outside of Bogotá was Arauca, a traditional ELN stronghold along the eastern border with Venezuela. The most tangible intersection of American involvement in Colombia's war, along with drugs, oil, guerillas, and to a significant degree child soldiers, Arauca had been under the sole control of the ELN for a long time. One of my closest friends and colleagues, photographer Stephen Ferry, accompanied me, as well as Ruth Morris, a British stringer for the *Los Angeles Times*, who went with us as my translator and "fixer" —someone who arranges logistical matters and meetings. She'd been based in Colombia a while and was pretty comfortable with the place. Because she was also a reporter, it was easy to communicate to her what I needed to do.

Stephen spoke Spanish fluently and had also been working in Colombia over several years. We'd met years before while working on a story about forensic anthropologists for *Life* magazine and had remained close ever since. Though it was our first time together in a conflict zone, I trusted his judgment unwaveringly.

We were looking for child soldiers and those who commanded them. What we found were adults and war-affected children who'd become adults, struggling to survive the legacies they had inherited. Several years earlier, the FARC started making moves into the area. It was notorious for kidnapping for cash, and my fears of our being taken hostage were justified shortly after my departure from the country, when Ruth and another photographer for the *Times* were indeed kidnapped. Fortunately, they were released unharmed after eleven days.

On our first of three nights, Stephen, Ruth, and I stayed in Saravena, and our baptism under fire came sometime after midnight. The three of us had rooms at a bare but comfortable hotel a short distance from downtown. The rooms had no televisions and no air conditioning or fans. For me it meant sleeping in boxers and a T-shirt, anxiously wondering if we would escape being kidnapped. Restless, I would drift in and out while listening to a Walkman, alternating with getting up and writing on a notepad.

I'd just drifted into a semi-sound sleep when the hits came. "Boom! Boom! Boom!" Dull explosions increasingly became sharp, and I leapt out of bed and put my ear to the door. I couldn't tell if the explosions were coming from mortars, but soon I made out the distinct sound of automatic rifle fire. "Are they trying to take the hotel?" I thought. After a few moments, I went to the balcony along the second floor where we slept, facing out onto an empty courtyard. Tracer rounds were being fired back and forth a short distance away. I was reminded of the summer light shows I used to love as a kid. Stephen was already outside watching, and Ruth joined us after a few minutes. The hotel seemed secure, but the heavy fighting was close by. The hotel's generator kept going out, an ominous occurrence that only fed my fears of the place being overrun by the guerillas. Silently, we listened to the shooting and sound of fireworks. Ruth went back to bed. Turning to Stephen, I asked him, half-seriously, "You wanna go out and see what's up?" My heart was racing, and if we were going to get into the thick of it during my time in Colombia, it might as well have been then. Turning to laugh, he replied, "Out there?"

The streets the next morning were eerily quiet when we ventured out. For the most part, the hotel had escaped serious damage, but refuse and spent shells lined the main streets of town. We came upon a young soldier in green fatigues standing in front of a collapsed building.

"What happened?" he asked in reply to Stephen's query. "What happened is what happens here. The militia attacked the police station and a couple of other buildings. Twice a week we're attacked, usually in groups of three. There were no casualties, this time. At first, people would lower their chins and not speak to us. It's hard to believe we all live in the same country."

Saravena is Colombia's so-called second city, located in Arauca, 220 miles northeast of Bogotá. The significance of Arauca to the United States stems from the Occidental Petroleum pipeline—owned by a Los Angeles corporation—running through it, in close proximity to an U'wa Indian reserve. The pipeline extends five hundred miles and is a favorite target for sabotage for the ELN. In late 2002, the U.S. Army sent Special Forces advisors to train Colombian infantrymen from two brigades in counter-insurgency, and incidentally to guard the pipeline.

That same year, President Uribe identified a "zone of resistance" across a wide swath of the nation. Inside of it, the state and military were given wide-ranging powers transcending traditional and political rights over 160,000 civilians across three provinces. This included warrantless searches, interception of telecommunication messages, movement restrictions, and seizure of property.

Our first stop was the local government military command. The visit was unexpected but ultimately worked in our favor given the rank of officer we were taken to see.

A major and second in command to General Rebei Pizzaro of the Mechanized Group Number 18 of the Eighteenth Brigade, William Bautista Castillo was most familiar with the operations of the ELN but had been forced to get quickly acquainted with FARC. Given the increased presence of FARC in Arauca, the ELN had begun providing information to the army in Saravena. The easygoing officer sat behind the wide wooden desk lined with cell phones, walkie-talkies, and a well-placed sno-globe of the Twin Towers. I liked him right away. He was formal, but not in an off-putting way. Regardless of whatever expressions he displayed, Castillo's eyes remained focused and warm.

He was thirty-two years old and had spent half his life in the Colombian army, having joined during a period when enlistment of minors was encouraged. An academic prodigy, the major was from Bogotá and received a scholarship to study in Germany. As an adult officer he became an expert in military planning and technology in Colombia and the United States.

Attending a cousin's graduation from military school, he heard the national anthem played by a full military band for the first time in his life and decided to join the army on the spot, leaving a university scholarship behind. When we met, it was his third tour of duty in Arauca. Behind him were a shelf with a row of flags, an ammo belt hanging off a coat rack, and a framed Colombian flag enclosed in glass. An air conditioning unit and overhead fan created a stark, cool environment in contrast to the dry, hot air outside. Major Castillo was more than happy to talk about the war in Colombia and the role of youth in it.

"The 'state of unrest' has made [us] more agile because we have more equipment and resources," he explained in reference to Uribe's then-new security measures. "Now we can take a census and the names of people who are coming and going in Saravena, as well as check vehicle registration and IDs. We have a prosecutor in town, but she can be pressured by one side or the other. Now, we can get permission for a search and seizure by fax." The tone in his voice hinted at a distrust of this prosecutor's role in the process.

"When you're confronting militias, it's not like [they] have a uniform on or a way of identifying them," he continued. "They're invisible, but these new measures help us to identify them." It had been three weeks since Uribe handed the military its expanded powers, and Castillo was pointing to significant results already. In Saravena and the surrounding area his division had made nineteen arrests and found a hiding place in a chicken coop that held ammunition, carbine rifles, and FARC propaganda.

Under the new provisions, people transporting gasoline or cement were required to get permission from Major Castillo. Because of the proximity to the border, most gasoline used in the zone was Venezuelan. Colombian gasoline can be three times the cost of that from Venezuela, in pesos. Dealing in contraband gasoline and cement is a precursor to cocaine trafficking.

"What we've learned about the ELN militias is that they typically have three areas of action divided into cells and mini-cells," said Castillo. "You can't compare their military capacity with the controlling front in the countryside. Children are usually used in the mini-cells."

Each cell has a leader, usually the head of a particular local militia. That leader will answer to someone on the rural front. As described by Major Castillo, a cell may have twenty people in it. Those twenty members might not be armed, but the leader will be and must supply food, rubber boots, and other necessities to those on the front line. The leader has the option of taking people out of unarmed, supply-oriented cells and putting them into military operations. Within these cells, two or three of the twenty members will be under eighteen years old and will be converted into *sicarios*, or assassins.

When the leaders bring cell members into the military branch, the members get training in the rural areas, even if they're urban. "In mini-cells, we've found children who have nothing else to do but participate in this," noted Castillo. "These recruits are used initially for intelligence purposes, spying.

"An urban military commander might tell one of these kids to get on a bicycle and go near the military areas to tell members of a [guerilla command] what they're doing, or carry messages. These kids also carry extortion notes. We call them 'Vikings,' after a popsicle brand.

"This is how young people can be moved up through the ranks, throughout a childhood. We've talked to people who've been involved in the war since they were five years old," he said, raising his voice to express disbelief.

It was in his discussion of FARC that Major Castillo expressed the least amount of understanding but the greatest concern. In close proximity to Saravena, within the Aurcua region, lies Charo Island, a strip of land between two rivers recently established as a FARC foothold. The island is well within the rehabilitation zone and is approximately nineteen miles by two miles, along a five-and-a-half-mile strip. Before the FARC faction's arrival, local Colombian farmers grew cocoa and exported it to the mainland from the island.

The FARC came and forced locals to grow coca, for processing into cocaine. The location has proven ideal for the rebels, given the island's fertility, accessibility for contraband gas, and opportunity for getting coca product out through Venezuela. The FARC ships out cocaine, and arms dealers send in weapons.

"There was heavy recruitment of children on that island," observed Castillo. "If you're a kid, the choices are pick coca leaves or become a militia member, and most of the pickers are children. We're talking about kids twelve years old and up. The FARC got to Charo Island about fifteen years ago and have been heavy in the area about half that time." It's difficult to do a military operation in Charo Island because of its proximity to the border. When a confrontation erupts, the FARC will escape beyond the army's reaches into Venezuela.

"People are really despairing there, because of pressure more than anything," said Castillo. "Those who collaborated with the FARC don't want to anymore because they see how the group destroys the town.

"There was a couple that came here two years ago from Cesar, another department. They opened a mechanic's shop and because they were different, they were murdered. The person who did it fits the profile of someone who joined young, then became a *sicario*. The young guy who joins a militia [ELN or FARC] in Saravena often doesn't have anything to do. They finish high school at seventeen, eighteen years old, and there's no work or opportunity to continue a career. Often, they're manipulated with power by being given a gun and told, 'You will collect extortion.' A motorcycle is given to them, and they're told to take a cut. Then, they may be told to attack an installation.

"There are a lot of expectations in the community regarding social spending, but [the money] hasn't arrived yet. The only way to break the cycle with the militias is constant government presence. Here, the government, the state, is army. I'm a small part of the state. The government has to be able to come here and offer great educational opportunities. Since these kids are small, they're injected with a [poor] view of authority. The only authority they see is the military. A few days ago I met with a group of about thirty teachers in high schools, and I told them we have to restore our values. A child from the beginning has to be taught respect for moral authority," explained Castillo, as if to say that was the fundamental basis for keeping kids out of the conflict.

LUÍS'S JOURNEY

According to "People on War," a study by the Committee International de la Croix Rouge (International Committee of the Red Cross)[4] in 1999, 82 percent of Colombians polled believe youth are not mature enough to fight until they are eighteen. Further, 70 percent believed that combatants who were too young had participated in the war. An overwhelming majority blamed these younger, less experienced fighters for continuing the fighting and committing abuses.

Before December 2000, some sixteen thousand youths under the age of eighteen had served in the Colombian armed forces. After protests from concerned public advocates and international groups, the government announced that this demographic group was no longer recruitable for combat but rather would be assigned office duties until they were eighteen years old. For the most part, that promise has been upheld, although army commanders continue to use kids as spies, as I saw firsthand after an army offensive in the Medellín *communas*.

Colombia did not afford special legal status or treatment to child soldiers. Children who were captured or surrendered could still be sent to trial before a special judge for juveniles or to a judge assigned to institutions for juvenile offenders. The process had been irregular for former child members of armed forces or groups when I was in Colombia, because of their unclear legal situation. More often than not, it was up to the discretion of a judge or commander whether a child soldier was tried or allowed to go directly for some type of assistance.

When former child soldiers try to leave armed groups by reporting to authorities, they may be required to collaborate and provide information about the armed groups and their commitment to them. Children can still receive the same treatment as adults in these situations, aside from being assigned a special judge.

Luckily for him, Luís ended up on a more stable, safe route when he left the war. The foot soldier went to FARC in 1997 after his parents, poor coffee and sugarcane farmers from the Huila department in the country's southwest, were shot to death by right-wing militiamen. The region is popular with narco-traffickers moving drugs from the country's interior to the coast. "There are old, indigenous caves leading from Huila to Cauca," explained Luís.

"My mother was a hard worker and very good at making stuffed pig," he told me proudly. "My father liked to help people. He had mules for rent to people carrying different cargo. My parents were killed because my father loaned a mule to a guerilla. All the neighbors left their homes running when they heard the shots. Someone in the community informed on him as a collaborator." That morning, annoyed at their son for accidentally drowning some chickens, Luís's parents sent him and his brother, then six, to an aunt's house—an act that saved both boys' lives.

Seeking vengeance, Luís offered his services to the rebels, who took him to their camp in the jungle near his village. There he found comradeship with other preteens and learned infantry skills—and discipline—from his elders. He and the other foot soldiers were fed ham, energy drinks, and other quick foods. Early in his stint he also met his first girlfriend, who would be killed in battle a year later.

"The FARC started me off easy, mostly with training and fighting," Luís recalled. "I had eight months of training. Sometimes the commanders would treat us well, sometimes poorly. If you got distracted 'Uncle' [the top commander] would berate you."

At fourteen he was promoted to bombmaker, or *ramplera*, crafting gas bombs and crude missiles for use against police stations and army bases. "I didn't get killed for two years, so they figured I knew how to take care of myself."

The gas bombs were made of fertilizer, gas, diesel fuel, and gunpowder. The teenager would meticulously break up particles of metal supports from houses and put them in the bombs for shrapnel. An electrical charge would set the device.

"It was dangerous work because you cannot mix the chemicals," he explained. "Being a *ramplera* was like a [promotion] and required a ten-month course. As you prepared the cylinders, they could go off and kill many."

Over time he discovered that the guerillas were as brutal—and as deeply involved in drug trafficking—as his parents' killers. "They asked me to kidnap and detain people. I didn't like to watch people held behind fences like cows. You start to think about it and how that could be you or one of your family members. How would they escape if the army attacked? It's badly done . . . not right . . . Everybody deserves their freedom. And when the wind blew wrong, my bombs sometimes landed in civilian houses. Even if they landed inside a police station, those were people just like me. Finally, I turned myself in because I got tired of doing what I shouldn't be doing."

Conscience-stricken, he fled to a local police station in the fall of 2001. When he was with the guerillas, they warned him of what happened to those who left their ranks, but once Luís had done it for himself, he saw things differently.

"I was going to turn myself in, but the army said they had captured me and I really didn't like that." He left the FARC on a sunny day, about ten in the morning. He was dressed in plain clothes, no uniform, but still wore the telltale rubber boots all the guerillas wore. He and a friend were at a gas station when the police arrived. They were searched but were without weapons.

"You know how they get soldiers from the army to infiltrate in the guerilla forces? Well, they had taken pictures of all of us, to the army and police. [They] had my picture. I was scared, since we're at war and they can always kill you.

"The police treated me OK, but the army didn't. The army would yell at us, asking us for the names of our commanders, and since we wouldn't tell them, they would treat us badly and harm us."

BIENESTAR FAMILIAR

After a few weeks in a detention center in Talima, Luís was taken to Bogotá and delivered to the main program in Colombia for former child soldiers, Bienestar Familiar, established in 1999 by the government and run by its Institute for Family Welfare.

When he arrived at the center after fighting for four years, it was the same as moving to a new home. Everything was different, calm. He had come from harsher, more hostile surroundings and had considerable adjustment problems as he seemed to fight with nearly everyone in sight.

I first met Luís at the center. Whenever I visited him and other kids there, a black Labrador mutt was always running around. It was a stray the kids had found and named Natalie Parees, after a Colombian model. Since the young veterans were more used to life in the countryside, the center was located in familiar surroundings, helping them readjust more easily to civilian life once their rehabilitation process was complete.

"I would hit everyone, and I did a lot of things, but I then learned that you can move forward and that in life you can achieve whatever you want," Luís told me. "When I first arrived I spent about six months being bad. Now, I can adapt anywhere. I can take my life wherever I want it to go."

Many of the youth served by the center change their physical appearances through weight and hair changes. "This is the best program available for these kids," explained Rommel Rojas, age thirty, a social worker with Bienestar. "These former combatants have lived in 'reduced worlds' where their exposure to armed groups comes little by little over time. They might join almost unconsciously, without knowing what the group is about." Most of the kids who come to Bienestar are FARC. There's never been a fifty-fifty mix of guerillas and paramilitary fighters.

According to Colombian law, the Bienestar Familiar program must be notified within thirty-six hours if a youth under the age of eighteen is in the custody of the national police or army. Child soldiers come to Bienestar by fleeing their comrades, being captured, or being turned over by a guerilla commander, which rarely happens. Once youths have been processed, they begin the three steps of the Bienestar curriculum. Right after demobilization they are supposed to stay in a *hogar transitorio*, or transitory home, for a month, where they are evaluated and given any immediate medical or psycho-social care. Depending on age and needs, they are assigned either to a household with five or six other kids and two adults or to a facility with up to thirty youngsters. They're taught reading, writing, and vocational skills and given counseling to help them cope with their traumas.

Following the *hogar transitorio*, a certain number of *desvinculados*, or ex–child soldiers, go to Benposta, a non-governmental organization that falls under the category of a CAE (Centro de Atención Especializada, or Center for Specialized Attention). After being in the rehabilitative center, the young person either returns home to a family or stays in a subsidized apartment.

At least a third of the youth assisted by Bienestar and Benposta are girls between the ages of thirteen and eighteen years old. No specific program deals with pregnancy, so girls are usually sent to foster homes to support them through their pregnancies. As Rojas, the Bienestar Familiar staff worker, explained to me, girls don't escape as often as boys do. The reasons could be fear, their differing perception of power, or simply a greater level of commitment to their group.

When I visited Bienestar's programs, two girls were living outside the regular, center-based system. Curious about the experience of girl soldiers in Colombia, especially those who'd gotten pregnant, I went to visit them at a secure space in Bogotá. One was a FARC fighter who had been captured, and the other had escaped from the ELN to deliver a baby boy.

The ELN soldier had delivered her child just three weeks before we met. She'd turned herself in to an army battalion in Pasto. As we spoke, she held a yellow blanket and overstuffed teddy bear in one arm and a light-olive-skinned baby boy in the other.

"My baby is a result of me being raped," the sixteen-year-old told me. "I had only been there for about two weeks, after being forced to go into the group. I hadn't been feeling well and suspected I was pregnant, but I was afraid they'd make me have an abortion. They might have even killed me for not being disciplined. Generally, they gave the girls birth control injections, but I hadn't been there long enough to get one. Also, I didn't agree with the injections because I didn't have a boyfriend. I didn't think this would happen to me. When I turned myself in, they gave me a pregnancy test because I was feeling dizzy and nauseated."

When she escaped, the frightened teenager went to her aunt's house and turned herself in to the army a short while later. Since going through Bienestar and having her child, she'd been in touch with the aunt and found out that the ELN was looking for her. I learned later that both girls managed to go home safely.

After two years the program helped put more than six hundred young men and women back into society. Most were turned over by the army after being captured, then evaluated by psychologists and social workers, and sent to one of sixteen rehabilitation facilities. There are eight centers and eight group homes run by Bienestar throughout Colombia. Every house has social workers, psychologists, teachers, and three or four assistants who help organize and care for the youths. Three of Bienestar's centers are named for characters from books by Gabriel García Márquez.

The reinsertion program for former child soldiers is overseen by three different government bodies: the Ministry of Defense, the Ministry of the Interior, and the Alto Comisionado de la Paz. All three constantly remain in turf wars and maintain their own strategies for dealing with mobilized youth. Unfortunately, one of the biggest drawbacks at Bienestar is that no follow-up system exists to track the youths who leave the program. Thus, there is no way of confirming whether the rehabilitation lasted or whether a child returns to fighting. In fact, the center where I first met Luís was eventually shut down after highly publicized criticism about its lack of oversight.

Release from the center is dependent on a judge's ruling on the youth's progress and situation at home. If the judge decides that the child is ready to go back into civilian society, the family can take the child back if it is safe. (In some situations the child's family is in an armed group.) Otherwise he or she is offered subsidized housing with other former child soldiers.

"We look at it on a case-by-case basis," explained Rojas in a conference room at Bienestar's headquarters in Bogotá, "asking how close they need to be to their families. By the time many of these kids have been recruited, they have usually had two or three years of school. When they get out, they're much older and don't want to be treated like kids by going to school with small ones. At the centers they get training and education for basic things, so at least they can read and write on a functional level."

"These aren't the kids most people have encountered—they've been in combat, had experience in kidnapping, and are surrounded by violence," noted Ludvia Serratao, a Bienestar social worker who was rotating among the centers when I visited. "Some of them have war wounds, even arriving in our system with bullets or shrapnel from grenades." The physical wounds would heal, but the inner ones could linger indefinitely.

SCARRED MINDS

Traveling to Colombia in order to understand the psychological consequences young people face during and after fighting, I met a handful who continued fighting battles away from the war zones, in their own heads. Going to Colombia introduced me to boys and girls numbed, scarred, and twisted by the violence of their lives. The violence in society, and the holes it created in the lives of young people, almost felt normal in Colombia.

Guillermo Carvajal, a member of the Colombian Psychoanalysis Society, focuses on the psychology of war. In his studies of the psychological impact of the war on Colombian youth, he noted that there are "two wars, one real and one imaginary. The first one is experienced from the outside, with concrete violent events. The second one is experienced exclusively in the mind, with violent mental objects generated by a violent environment." Further, the way war affects a young person depends on his or her relation to it. For example, Carvajal sees those who've been nurtured to have the "warrior frame of mind" as being very different from others who endure constant mental trauma as a result of being victimized through displacement, physical wounding, or imagery.[5]

Sadly, the war in Luís's mind was all too real. He developed a habit of cutting his own arms with scissors or shards of glass shortly after arriving at the Bienestar's group center. "With all of his losses," said psychologist Erika Romero, who rotated among Bienestar centers and visited different children across Colombia, "he'd never gone through the process of grieving. As a guerilla he could take out his pain against the world. Now that's not possible. He has to punish himself." After nine months of therapy and a heavy regimen of antidepressants, the cutting stopped. "I think of what has happened as a test life gave me," Luís said. "If I weren't [at the center], I'd be dead or putting my life at risk. The challenge for me is to build a better future." I learned to my dismay that after my initial visits with Luís, the cutting resumed briefly. No one said it outright, but my guilt led me to take the blame for leading him back to the traumatic memories of his guerilla fighting with the FARC.

Part of the therapy used at Bienestar employed the magical realism of García Márquez to look at dreams. Romero told me Luís's journals, which I did not read, were full of self-reflection. Because of the limitations with his writing, he dictated his words to a staff member, usually someone skilled to deal with the psycho-social issues he faced.

Nearly two years after we first met, Luís had moved to a new place, living with four other Bienestar boys in a cabin. He was studying electricity, crafts, hygiene, and construction. Once all his vocational classes were completed, Luís was going to be evaluated for job placement. The new Bienestar center close to where he lived had an experimental agricultural program that Luís liked, and his days were divided between farming in the morning and school courses from noon until 5 PM. He didn't leave the center that often except to hang out in the park with his friends.

"The good things at Bienestar are that they taught me manners and respect, because you have none of that when you're fighting," he noted. "There are many reasons and justifications why someone would decide to enlist with the guerillas. It all depends on his family situation. I didn't have anything to live off, so I went. Also, you're there to fight for a cause, but we were never going to get to live out their cause, because they want to take over and that will never happen. I believed in the cause when I entered, because you go in blind, and only when you leave and talk to other people do you realize that everything is very different.

"Sometimes I feel rage toward [the FARC]," he continued. "I think that when I leave the center, I could be killed, because when I turned myself in, I turned in my rifle and equipment. For them, that's a big offense. There are sixty FARC fronts. They talk to each other and know me. I don't like the city; I like the countryside. I like to work the land. I grew up in the countryside. I can't return there because all my family members are in the guerilla forces, and if I go, they'll kill me."

"ETC."

I encountered a number of youths who were former child soldiers, but I didn't meet any who had been actively fighting for weeks until Stephen, Ruth, and I traveled to infamous Medellín. There we found a city with a number of young men who'd been killers for much of their short lives. Just before my visit, a confrontation between the paras and the guerillas took place in front of a Medellín school. A teacher at the school had to come out and negotiate a fifteen-minute cease-fire so that her students could make it out of the building and go home.

On average there are nearly three hundred murders a month in Medellín; by comparison, Chicago averages fifty per month. So I shouldn't have been surprised when several automatic weapon rounds came through my hotel window one night, slamming the wall above the bed where I lay reading, shattering the window, and scaring the hell out of me.

During our visit to the city, the Colombian government launched the biggest urban offensive in the history of the war, "Operation Orion," against a guerilla stronghold known as Communa 13. Seventy-five percent of Colombia's population lives in urban areas, and increasingly the conflict with the guerillas has moved to the cities. In Medellín the FARC held a great advantage in numbers and power within key neighborhoods. Ultimately, thirty child soldiers were sent to Bienestar Familiar after capture in Operation Orion. Ruth and I had stayed behind to do some follow-up interviews in Bogotá, and Stephen went ahead to Medellín, while Operation Orion was in full force.

"Prior to this operation, there had been short forays by the police into those main neighborhoods where the guerillas are based," a national police officer explained to me a day after Orion ended. "This time, the police decided to push in and hold the area. The guerillas were used to the police launching these quick operations, but when it came time for the long haul, they couldn't hold their neighborhoods and repel the government forces."

When the major fighting eased, Stephen, Ruth, and I traveled to the western part of the city where Orion had been focused. It was labyrinthine, with twisting, narrow streets strewn with trash and human refuse. Redbrick hovels were jaggedly stacked atop one another. Spray-painted messages emblazoned most walls. "Get out murderous army, yesterday you killed fighters, today you killed children," read one. Black crows loitered on the roofs of smoldering buildings. It was a guerilla area, at least in terms of community sympathy.

We came upon some young men sitting in front of a small grocery. Curious about our presence there, they started chatting, and one youth wearing a red Coca-Cola hat did an improvisational rap for us. The neighborhood was called "the Hole."

One teenager put his fingers up to his head like a gun. "This is the only way out," he said with a smile.

"So you writing about life here?" another one asked me.

"I'm trying to," I replied.

"Well, you could write a whole book about violence in this neighborhood and end it with etc., etc., etc.," chimed in another.

A fifteen-year-old girl had been one of the many minors taken into custody during Orion. Captured in a *communa* called "20 del Julio," she was caught guarding a university student who'd been kidnapped for ransom. Stephen, Ruth, and I went to the *sijin*, or local jail, to find her.

It was an overcrowded compound of blue-and-white, one- and two-story buildings with stucco roofs. In the center was a grassy area with palm trees. On one side mopeds and motorbikes were parked against a wall, and official SUVs and trucks lined the other. The grassy area had white benches and stone memorial plaques for soldiers and police from that precinct who'd been killed.

Outside, a crowd of women and small children stood with a few old men among them. These were the wives, children, and relatives of those who had been detained and accused of being guerillas. Nearly everyone held packages of food and blankets for their loved ones inside. The smell of meat with rice (*empanadas*) and other savory dishes wafted through the group. A restaurant just outside the *sijin*'s gates, "Cafeteria y Restaurante Laslomas Sijin," was doing brisk business, even in the pitch-black night.

After hours of waiting and tip-toe negotiation, the three of us arranged to meet with some teenagers held inside, though the fifteen-year-old girl we originally sought had been moved elsewhere already. The next morning, two teenagers named Juan Carlos and Hido were brought into an extraordinarily cramped interviewing room just outside the main holding cells. There was just enough space for the two boys, Ruth, and me on flimsy white plastic chairs. A low fluorescent light made the brown-and-green tiled floor look the color of vomit. Just outside the entrance, plain-clothes police officers with obvious bulges under their shirts watched us carefully, particularly interested in the thick notebook in my hand.

The two youths were from Bente de Julio barrio, in Communa 13, but hadn't known each other before being put in the same group cell. Juan Carlos, age seventeen, wore a pinstriped, button-down shirt, red shorts, and black sneakers with no socks or laces. He opened the shirt to proudly reveal a heart tattoo emblazoned on his right shoulder. Juan Carlos lived with his girlfriend and six-month-old child, who had been named after him. "You have to leave a namesake in case the army kills you," he explained. He claimed to be at home washing dishes when soldiers broke in to take him, based on the word of an informant who ratted him out to police.

"Every time they come to my neighborhood, they come to my house!" he said incredulously. "There are witnesses who saw them take me, this time. I was grabbed around the neck and hit in the face. See how loose my tooth is? In my area, there's always a lot of gunfire from the militias there."

The full-service kitchen served only officers and other personnel, so prisoners would eat only if their families brought them food or another detainee was feeling generous. Juan Carlos's grandmother had brought rice and beans, which he willingly shared with his cellmates. "My grand-mother doesn't like my girlfriend because she's a racist," he said. "My girlfriend is black. If I get out of here, I'd like to go live with her in the Santo Domingo barrio. She works with nuns taking care of invalid kids. Her family will take care of us."

As he spoke, I noticed how nervous Hido seemed. I attributed it to the circumstances of his situation, until Ruth, catching my eye, took my pad and wrote down "egg beater." That seemed to be a nickname for a guerilla. Given Hido's denials of having done anything wrong, I took it to mean that Juan Carlos was in fact somehow tied to the group, and Hido was not.

Hido seemed small and thin inside the grey sweatshirt and shorts he wore. His peach-fuzz mustache was almost comical, as did a flat-top hair-cut. I felt sorry for him. Hido betrayed the slack demeanor of a stoner (he'd started smoking pot at age eleven). He'd had to move to a different neighborhood after a friend had been knifed. Living at home with his mom, he wasn't in school but did work a regular job. He was angry for being locked up mostly because it meant missing work.

"Because we're from Communa 13, we don't have any rights here," he proclaimed. "I'm not that scared because I didn't have anything to do with this militia stuff. I am concerned about the situation inside this place. This morning is the first time we were fed since I arrived. And imagine being in the same sweat and clothes for days!"

It was unclear whether the two would be sent to Bienestar or returned home. Neither they nor anyone in their cell had been formally charged or told what they'd been accused of doing. Over the next few days, they hoped, a judge would release them.

As we left the interview room and walked past the cafeteria, I noticed a strange sight. Three individuals were sitting inside, beneath a mute televi-sion set hanging from a wall corner. One woman, one older boy, and another slight figure in a green mask, blue shirt, and orange pants were eating and drinking sodas. They turned out to be informants. The one behind the mask was fourteen.

Despite the hot, breezy day, he kept the mask on. When Stephen asked why he was helping the army and police, he replied "because the militias threatened my mom. I want to help make the community a better place."

If life is difficult for most Colombian youth, it is nearly a dead end for one living in Medellín, which has 60 percent malnutrition and employment rates. Humanitarian groups estimate that seven thousand young people in Medellín are involved with one of the three main fighting groups. Pablo Escobar and his cronies created legions of young assassins in Medellín's barrios. After Escobar's group left, the paras came in and disciplined them. Because the law is so lax with minors, the militias and the paramilitaries exploited them with an unsettling regularity.

Medellín was a wild trip. There, with Stephen, I had some of the most edgy encounters I have ever had in my life. By day we'd hang out with coked-up kids with guns; at night we'd blow most of our money at casinos or drinking at restaurants in the posh *Zona Rosa.*

Being in Medellín also served as a cruel reminder of how devalued a life could be in Colombia. Riding in a taxi one afternoon en route to a meeting with a local contact, we saw the driver in front of us get out and chase his passenger down the street. Curious, Stephen and I exited our car, leaving Ruth alone with the driver. A block down the street, a wiry young guy was being pummeled by a growing crowd. The driver we'd seen giving chase was in the middle, slapping the kid's bare back with the blade of a machete. Apparently he hadn't paid or hadn't paid enough. The circumstances didn't really matter. Violence was in the air and everyone wanted a part of it. Stephen and I had the bright idea of pulling the guy out of there. But no sooner did Stephen reach out and grab the poor man than we were both surrounded.

I panicked, thinking it was our turn to be beaten, but a police van pulled up, and several officers jumped out and grabbed the victim. In less than a minute, the police, the man, and the crowd were all gone. Finding a dark comic relief in the situation, Stephen and I started laughing and walked back to Ruth and the increasingly impatient driver.

On another slow afternoon, Stephen and I found ourselves in Medellín without Ruth, who had gone to Bogotá for another assignment. I had written all the notes I could and took a late-morning nap. Around lunchtime Stephen wanted to go into the main downtown square to take pictures and asked me to go along with him.

We ended up at a fruit stand a short distance from our hotel. Stephen was photographing people, and I stood behind him trying to look more intimidating than I felt. One of the vendors started getting nervous and put a paper bag over his head to prevent Stephen from photographing him.

"You don't have to do that," Stephen told him reassuringly with an amused smile. "We're not with the police; we're journalists."

"What if he decides to start killing people?" said paper-bag man, pointing at me. In a situation where even the most familiar faces can be a threat, a nerdy black guy wearing glasses could be mistaken for an assassin.

Several days before we left Medellín for Bogotá and a flight back home, my hotel room was hit by stray gunfire from one of the neighboring *communas*. I had dozed off reading a magazine with the television on in the corner; I woke up to glass from my window breaking into the room and my bed sliding away from the wall. I hadn't heard the shots, but I could see the hole in the wall behind me. It was a few hours past midnight, but I went to get Stephen. I had to knock on his door for several minutes before he answered, bleary-eyed.

Into his half-awake face I exclaimed, "I think someone just shot at me!"

He came across the hall into my room and pulled the curtains back to reveal the shattered window and torn-up wall.

"You wanna sleep on my floor tonight?" he offered.

"Naw, I'm gonna stay here," I replied defiantly. I wasn't going to let anyone force me out of my room, gunshots or not.

I spent the rest of the night on the hardwood floor of my room and had the lightest sleep I could ever remembering having. The next morning, Stephen and I went to tell the concierge what had happened. A small group of desk clerks and porters gathered around the front desk to listen. I caught a few smirking out of the corner of my eye, but the concierge seemed sincerely concerned and surprised.

"Gentlemen, I can assure you this has *never* happened before!" he argued.

Although violence and danger were ever-present, the time we spent in Medellín was somehow incredibly invigorating. It was there that I fell in love with the Colombians. Despite decades of violence and war, despite the crippling poverty that virtually imprisoned people from birth, I was still able to find conflict-affected youth in Medellín who managed to maintain the light of hope in the face of unremitting darkness.

GUESO

Across the city from guerilla-leaning Communa 13 lived one of the most tragic young people I met during my time in Colombia, Gueso, a child soldier who was still fighting. He proudly served with the Cacique Nutibara Block, a paramilitary militia in San Pablo with approximately three hundred fighters, eighty of whom were under the age of eighteen. Gueso joined in 2001 but had known the group's commander, Piolin, for some time. He learned how to use his first weapon—a .38 pistol—at eight years old, which is how the spindly soldier quickly honored his nom de guerre, which means "gun" in local slang. Sixteen years of living in San Pablo, one of hundreds of hillside *communas* surrounding downtown Medellín, made him first into a cold-blooded gang assassin and then a die-hard foot soldier.

Commander Piolin, or "Martin," as he was typically called in the neighborhood, was pragmatic about the use of kids as soldiers. Joining a street gang at the age of twenty, he rose to a position of authority in the neighborhood and Medellín as a whole. One of his uncles had been killed by the FARC. In many ways Piolin held together AUC factions that normally wouldn't get along. Before Gueso's arrival at the store for our meeting, Piolin explained to me the necessity of children's taking up arms in the midst of war.

In Piolin's description of the process, it was easy to mistake the whole thing as recruitment and training for a jobs program for youth instead of one that turned children into stone-cold killers. He was polished and looked more like a hip businessman than commander. Wearing white khaki pants, grey sneakers, and a blue-purple dress shirt, he exuded cool, with no hairs out of place and no stress lines on his face. A silver watch gleamed on one wrist, and an unusually large gold ring graced the index finger of his left hand. He spoke calmly, but I never saw him look directly at me, except when he thought I wasn't looking. Otherwise, he constantly scanned the corner and watched Gueso with his friends across the street. Stephen and I suspected they were snorting or smoking something whenever they disappeared out of our sight.

Midway through the interview, Piolin paused to intervene in a personal dispute on the street with two women being harassed by a man. It was immediately obvious the power he held, even among those who weren't children fighting alongside him. "Here the community looks to us to solve the problems," he noted. "Why do they look to us rather than the authority? Because the authority doesn't give them solutions to their problems."

As he spoke, we watched the bustling intersection the store faced. People were washing cars, kids were soliciting money for their school groups, and families were working on the outsides of their homes.

"Usually kids come to this fighting life through a friend," observed Piolin. "There will be some kind of a test. Let's say a person has never killed anyone. Before they can join, the group will have them kill. They join us between the ages of thirteen and seventeen years old, in general. I have about ten minors with me, but I am trying to correct that problem. We'll call them at home or talk to their parents and start at C.V. It includes information on whether they've killed anyone, general behavior, drug use, their extent of schooling, etc. Many people want revenge because they've had a cousin or friend killed in the fighting, for example. But we want people who are more in line with us politically and motivated by those reasons.

"An older person is more reserved to put themselves in the thick of it," he continued, while sipping on a bottle of Malta, a popular malted drink. "A young person doesn't think of anything, doesn't think about his family. He's only thinking about the objective."

Listening incredulously, I couldn't believe when the assured soldier told me of a program for all of his fighters, which I'd never heard of taking place anywhere else in the world. According to him, the AUC paid professional psychologists to come in and work with the kids on speaking and behavioral skills in dealing with civilians. "In war, you have to look out for everything," Piolin explained. Later, spending time with Gueso, I couldn't help wondering what exactly it involved.

A short time after my first conversation with Piolin, outside the same corner store in his neighborhood, I sat with Gueso on a mild Friday afternoon. Black army helicopters flew in the distance. It was the end to an eventful week both for him and for the city-at-large because of Operation Orion. The night before, he had been in uniform and on guard duty in the neighborhood. Around three o'clock in the morning, Gueso and another soldier spotted guerillas driving into the area with the intention of setting off a car bomb. There had been warning ahead of time, so Gueso and his companion shot up the vehicle and everyone inside.

His blood red eyes were dilated, beneath a bowl haircut that gradually faded to a buzz on the sides. He readily admitted that he used cocaine, cigarettes, and alcohol. He was scrawny, visibly wired, and none too intimidating. Gueso seemed curious about my inability to fully converse in Spanish. I could talk to him about music—rap and Metallica were his favorites—but the fact that he was high and armed made me nervous. "Ecstasy or synthetic drugs are no-no's because you lose the five senses," he explained, overlooking the same effect from his cocaine habit.

The scars covering his body were a testament to the dangerous life he had already lived. A dull red scar ran horizontally along his neck at shoulder level. An index finger was bulbous and swollen, resembling a mangled knob. A bullet remained embedded in his foot.

"There are shootings every night here," he told me. "Those that don't know how to fight die around here." Three years before, he had shot several guerillas dead in the very spot where he now sat.

Through dilated eyes he spoke fast and proudly of his wounds, pointing out each with a gruesome background story. As he introduced me to his fellow young fighters and walked around, his thoughts and proclamations sounded like an indistinguishable torrent, as if he had to get everything out. "When I was nine and a half, I stabbed a guy in the neck," he said, smiling. "He was my sister's boyfriend. At ten and a half years I was stabbed in the arm with a shiv [knife]. Then, we were in a fight with some ELN militia, and they captured me at fourteen. They asked me where my boss was. I said, 'I don't have a boss.' They said, 'Your boss is Piolin.' When they saw they couldn't do anything to make me talk, someone put a nylon wire around my neck and hit me in the knee with a whip. I had to kill the guy who was guarding me with a knife. You always have a knife with you. So I ran away and took a taxi to get home. I also have a bullet in my foot."

I often had to ask the same questions of Gueso, at different points in time, never being sure of his short life's chronology of violence and chaos. The drugs and his inability to focus had definitely affected his memory. Maybe that was the point.

More than a few times he told Stephen and me, "Sometimes I feel like killing."

The youngest of seven kids, he left home because of disagreements with his mother, who couldn't tolerate drug use or killing people. Gueso's father died of a heart attack when Gueso was nine years old. "[My mother] says we can talk after I've quit drugs," Gueso recalled. "I didn't get on with her. She wouldn't give me food, and she would hit me. She says, 'When they kill you, I'll pick up your body and bury you, and I'll cry for you.' She's very angry at me."

He would occasionally take groceries to Piolin's house or receive clothes and sneakers. Eventually, he was recruited to do guard duty and then later to go after guerillas. "I was in a training course for two weeks, not that far from here," he said. "On the weekends I wear civilian clothes, but on weeknights I'm in uniform. My job is also to kill [guerillas]. We know who they are by their appearance. Yellow shoes, damaged teeth, torn clothes, tangled hair. They look like hippies. Some nights your finger gets so sore from pulling the trigger. I would say I've killed about six or seven. We've got an eight-year-old kid with us too. He fires like crazy in a firefight!"

Like many youth caught up as child soldiers, Gueso shared a paternalistic relationship with his commander, whom he held in the highest regard. "To him, I'm like a pet, like a son, because I'm serious and honest," he explained. "If I have something to tell someone, I don't say it to their back. [Piolin] is like a dad for me. He understands people. You ask him for a favor, and he does it right away."

From Piolin's point of view, the fighting gave youth a sense of family their own blood relatives or society could not. "These kids don't have human warmth in their home environments," he said. "To look at the problem, start with family. Lots of them come up to me and say, 'Commander, you give me the affection my own father doesn't.'" A former gang member himself, he came from a background much like that of his charges. He gave them clothes and occasionally money to supplement their soldiers' pay—for Gueso, $30 every month or two. "The government is to blame for not giving the young people an education and jobs. Besides, the guerillas are against the community."

The AUC and associated factions such as the Cacique Nutibara had learned much from watching the opposing guerillas in their control of neighborhoods throughout Medellín. Typically, the guerillas levied a tax on taxis and buses, as well as on many other regular jobholders in the *communas*. "You can have a thousand men, but if you don't have the support of the community, you don't have anything," Piolin explained. "We don't charge taxes." Instead, they received their guns and munitions from the larger AUC division and made money from drugs or the creation of sanitation and other jobs. "You can't fight a war with a bake sale and raffles!" he added.

"It's not that I don't feel bad about [kids fighting]," Piolin said. "It's not that I want them to be in this, but it's a necessity. If it were up to me, the situation wouldn't be like this. We're stuck with the war. The guerillas have left a bad taste in people's mouths. There are people who are fighting for both sides because they don't know what they're fighting for. We're fighting against the guerillas because they're against this community, and we recognize that the guerillas were formed to fight on behalf of the people, but they have lost their vision. They say they want to supplant the state, but why attack the people?"

Gueso's own feelings about his life and outlook for the future were decidedly pessimistic. In his short life there had been few examples of someone getting out of the fighting or living a long time in it.

Piolin had offered to send Gueso back to school, if he wanted it. But having dropped out because of threats from guerilla sympathizers there, he'd decided not to go back. "No one here says they don't want to study," said Gueso of he and the other youth in his unit. "Piolin offered me a chance, but I told him, 'If I didn't study when I was in school, why would I study now?'"

After a week of hanging out with him and his friends, our final conversations were all tinged with melancholy, as if we both doubted the chances of seeing each other again. Early one bright morning, Stephen and I went to say goodbye and talk one last time in the regular meeting place, the corner store. Across the street, a group of young men washed a yellow taxi with the car doors open. A song by Dr. Dre played on the car stereo, echoing through the neighborhood. Gueso rose from a chair to greet us and then moved over to his friends, pitching in on the car-washing and stuffing the metallic radio in the pocket of his shorts.

At the café where we always met, an old man would listen to our conversations whenever I came to the neighborhood. "It's as if God and the Devil walked together," he whispered softly about Gueso. I nodded and turned to watch Gueso with his friends. After a few minutes I walked over to join him. I asked him what he felt inside, given all the things he'd done as an assassin, then a soldier. From the days we'd spent hanging out, I felt that he needed me to understand him and maybe not to judge.

"I'm not a soldier or anything; I'm just normal," he stammered. "I do these things because I want to. When you kill someone, you do feel weird inside. You look around and feel like everyone is looking at you, like the police are going to get you. It's never easy—it's always at a cost. It's the impression of what you've seen when a guy falls down, how a body moves when a bullet enters. It stays recorded in your head. When it's my turn to die, I'll die.

"I believe in God and the Sacred Virgin," he told me. "But after death, I don't know. Maybe I'll burn in hell. Who knows? Those of us fighting can't enter into eternal rest because of the bad things we did in the war. Sometimes I'll be sitting at home asking why I'm in this, and it makes me angry. But you can't leave. Your friends might kill you."

In November 2003, the Cacique Nutibara Block was ostensibly demobilized. The government was making good on a promise to disarm the paramilitary groups, bring them under tighter control of the government, or both. Eight hundred soldiers handed over their weapons to government authorities. There were several statements on behalf of the *communa* residents that the weapons given up were not those used by the paras in their area. Residents noted that several of the heads of the Nutibara Block did not turn themselves in. They also alleged that those weapons were taken from people's homes and handed in. Unfortunately, there was no specific oversight process that ensured that the soldiers didn't rearm themselves.

According to the Peace Commissioner's Office, forty-eight children were demobilized, and 570 weapons were handed over. There was no way of knowing if Gueso was one of the forty-eight. If he wasn't, the odds of his still being alive as a fighter for the AUC are small, but thinking about the vacancy in his eyes and the sad, twisted smile he would flash while carrying that radio around, I hope so. I keep thinking about one of the last things he said to me: "I'm not afraid to die, but I'm afraid to die so young. You can't think about the future here, because the future is a coffin."

NOTES

1. Laura Barnitz, Jimmie Briggs, Frank Smyth, and Rachel Stohl, "Colombia: No Safe Haven from War," Youth Advocate Program International Resource Paper, July 11, 2001, p. 2.

2. Beatriz Linares, "Demobilizing and Protecting Children Affected by the Armed Conflict," paper presented at The War's Children Symposium, Convenio de Buen Tratro, Programa Presidencial de Derechos Humanos y Derecho Internacional Humanitario, August 24, 2000.

3. Barnitz et al., "Colombia," 3.

4. "People on War: Country Report Colombia," by Greenberg Research, Inc., for the International Committee of the Red Cross Worldwide Consultation on the Rules of War, November 1999, p. 11.

5. Guillermo Caraval, "Children Made for War," paper presented at The War's Children Symposium.

(Top) The remains of several hundred Tutsi civilians who were massacred during the country's 1994 genocide were exhumed and reburied as a memorial to the victims of genocide in Kaduha in 1995. Hundreds of thousands of Rwandan children died as a result of the genocide and war. *Copyright © 1995 Corinne Dufka*

(Bottom) A boy with a machete scar on the back of his head, caused by being attacked at the height of the genocide, stands with other children outside the Cyugaro primary school near the town of Nyamata. In an area where hundreds died in ethnic fighting, the school teaches children from both the Hutu and Tutsi ethnic groups. *Copyright © 1994 Betty Press/UNICEF*

(Top) Two prisoners stand outside the gates of Gikondo Central Prison in Kigali. Due to a lack of money and staff, prisoners are assigned essential duties like security. There have been surprisingly few escapes. *Copyright © 1999 Damaso Reyes*

(Bottom) Ten years after the genocide, with his wife and young son in the background, François Minani sits in front of his hillside home in Gitarama speaking about the problems he has encountered finding work to support his wife and young son since his parents died.
Copyright © 2004 Damaso Reyes

The hand of a former guerilla fighter for the ELN who was fifteen when the explosive he was assembling detonated. He also lost an eye in the accident.

Copyright © 2002 Sebastian Brett/ Human Rights Watch

Bedroom of a former child combatant in a home run by the Bienestar Familiar.

Copyright © 2002 Joanne Mariner/Human Rights Watch

Sign posted in 2000 on the outskirts of San Vicente del Caguan, a town controlled by the FARC, saying: "Don't mistreat children; they are the future—FARC-EP."

Copyright © 2002 Joanne Mariner/Human Rights Watch

(Top) "Gueso," a member of the Cacique Nutibara faction of the AUC paramilitary group, stands on patrol in Medellín. *Copyright © 2002 Stephen Ferry*

(Bottom) The identity card of Ida Carmelita being held by her mother, Sebastiana Figerardo. *Copyright © 1999 Rebecca Shavulsky*

The mother of Ida Carmelita, Sebastiana Figerardo, at her family home in Mannar, standing in the living room where Ida was raped and murdered.

Copyright © 1999 Rebecca Shavulsky

Nixon, who joined the Tamil Tigers at the age of 14 and lost his leg soon afterward, sits in a room at the Bandarawela Bindunawarena Rehabilitation Center rehabilitation camp.

Copyright © 1999 Rebecca Shavulsky

(Top) Former child soldiers assemble at the Bandarawela Bindunawarena Rehabilitation Center for Tamil Tigers, run by the Sri Lankan government. *Copyright © 1999 Rebecca Shavulsky*

(Bottom) In Uganda, a former child soldier who escaped from the rebel Lord's Resistance Army (LRA) sweeps the sandy ground in front of a tent at the Gulu Save the Children Organization (GUSCO) reception center, in the town of Gulu in the district of the same name. A bandage on the boy's knee covers a wound he sustained during captivity. *Copyright © 2004 Chulho Hyun/UNICEF*

The Rachele Rehabilitation Center in Lira, northern Uganda, works with children abducted by the Lord's Resistance Army (LRA) to give them psycho-social counseling, medical treatment, and help reintegrating them back into society. As part of their counseling, the children reenact their abduction with some playing the role of the Uganda People's Defence Forces, some playing the role of LRA rebels, and some playing the role of civilians. It is estimated that 85 percent of the LRA are children forcibly indoctrinated, some of them spending years in captivity before managing to escape. The LRA wants to overthrow the current government and rule Uganda by the Ten Commandments and has been fighting a civil war for the past 18 years.

Copyright © 2004 Vanessa Vick

Charlotte Awino, 22, was one of the 139 students abducted from Saint Mary's College Aboke on October 10, 1996, by the Lord's Resistance Army (LRA). One hundred and nine girls where released immediately after their abduction to Sister Rachele Fassera, a

nun who worked at the school, but the remaining 30 where still held hostage by the LRA. In the past year, ten of the Aboke girls have managed to escape and four are known to have been killed. Six girls have still not been accounted for, and it is not known if they are alive, if they remain in the custody of the rebels, or if they are dead. Charlotte managed to escape on July 19, 2004, after eight years in captivity. During that time, she was forced to marry an LRA commander and had two children with him, Ronald Rubanga Kene, 5, and Miracle, 2. Charlotte's mother, Anjelina Atyam, has become known internationally for bringing attention to the plight of children in northern Uganda. *Copyright © 2004 Vanessa Vick*

(Top) Sergeant Nathan Ross Chapman, the first American to die in combat during Operation Enduring Freedom, in January, 2002. *Copyright © United States Deparment of Defense, Special Forces Branch*

(Center) A man shows posters that illustrate different trades to Mohammed Amin, 18, a former child soldier, during a job counseling session in a school in Charikar, capital of the Central Region province of Parwan. Mohammed, who is in the process of being demobilized, served as a runner in a rebel group for two years. He wanted to go to school but joined an armed group to help support his family. He is now participating in the UNICEF-supported demobilization program. Several schools have been designated as demobilization points. *Copyright © 2004 Kate Brooks/UNICEF*

(Bottom) Raqib, 18, a former child soldier, descends the stairs at a school in the Central Region province of Parwan. He is carrying his oath to respect the social norms of the community and make a positive contribution to its development. The oath is taken near the end of the UNICEF-supported demobilization process. Raqib will now complete the process by changing into civilian clothes and turning in his weapon. *Copyright © 2004 Kate Brooks/UNICEF*

3

A Woman's War:
Sri Lanka and the Tamil Tigers

HAD IDA CARMELITA not become a member of the Liberation Tigers of Tamil Eelam (LTTE), it would have been nothing short of a miracle. Based in Sri Lanka, LTTE, also known as the Tamil Tigers, is one of the fiercest, most feared guerilla groups in the world. The youngest of Sebastiana Figerardo's seven children, Ida was the second to join the rebels in their long-running war for autonomy against the Sri Lankan government. The family lived on Mannar Island on the eastern coast of Sri Lanka, a region known for its tenuous wooden perches on narrow poles high above the ocean, on which Sri Lankan men sit for hours on end, catching fish for their families to eat, as well as to sell. Ida's father died less than a month after she was born, leaving Sebastiana to raise seven children alone.

Even if Sebastiana had not been a widow, survival would have been difficult for her and the children. Often they went without regular meals. But

Sebastiana kept the children alive and out of the civil war, which erupted in 1983 when Ida was five. The dream that her children would be educated and would survive to raise their own families kept her going. It would never be more than a dream.

In 1990, when Ida was twelve, she was sent to India while her mother and siblings stayed behind. Sending daughters and sons to nearby India was not uncommon, especially as the fighting escalated. It was easier for a child to travel alone than for the whole family to endure the trek across the Indian Ocean. In Tamil Nadu, India, where many Sri Lankans in the north had family, acquaintances, or contacts, opportunities for a life of peace and some advancement existed. The war at home made the semblance of a normal life impossible. Ida lived in various refugee camps for over a year but did receive schooling until the assassination of Indian Prime Minister Rajiv Gandhi at the hands of a Sri Lankan suicide bomber. From that point on, no Sri Lankan refugees were allowed to be schooled. Ida drifted in India for a while before returning to Mannar in 1994.

Within a month she witnessed the murder of two of her brothers at home by members of a paramilitary government-aligned Tamil group known as TELO. Her brothers were slightly older than Ida, but still teenagers. Attempting to save them, their mother had been shot in the hip.

Two other brothers were also lost because of the murder. One was mentally traumatized and began showing psychotic behavior. The other, Napoleon, joined the LTTE.

Fearful that Ida was vulnerable, Sebastiana moved her outside of Mannar to a nearby village in the hopes of keeping her in school, but instead she delivered her right into the rebels' hands. Learning of her brothers' fate, the local LTTE enticed her to join them in fighting to avenge their deaths. So in 1996, seventeen-year-old Ida Carmelita left her family to spend the next three years as a guerilla soldier for the Tamil Tigers. She would barely live to see twenty-one—not because of a battlefield wound, but because she was gang-raped and tortured in the living room of her family's home. Her story mirrors that of thousands of other girls in Sri Lanka who have been forcibly recruited or who join to protect themselves against economic hardship and rape. In Ida's case, that protection would be brutally turned on its head.

————

Tear-shaped, Sri Lanka is a lush, agriculturally rich nation known for its production of tea, mangos, spices, and seafood. Perhaps the greatest resource of all are its scenic coastlines. The beaches in the south of the country draw surfing enthusiasts from all over the world, and European tourists flock year-round to the colonial-style estates in existence since before the British left in the late 1950s. A significant number of foreign travelers accounted for the tragically high death toll following the devastating tsunami that hit South Asia in December 2004.

At the same time that people from around the world have been venturing to Sri Lanka for a genteel holiday, a harrowing battle between Hindu Tamils seeking a separate, independent state and the ruling Buddhist Sinhala government has claimed the lives of over sixty thousand civilians and displaced an estimated six hundred thousand from their homes since 1983. Tamils comprise nearly one-sixth of the country's 18.6 million people. Many Tamil children have been recruited or conscripted into the LTTE cadres and drawn into combat. Others have endured or witnessed torture, rape, or murder at the hands of government forces.

The Tamil Tigers have waged a hugely successful campaign employing conventional warfare, guerilla hit-and-run attacks, and suicide bombings—even though they are vastly outnumbered by the government's forces. The alienation of language, religion, and nationality has forged a deep rift between the Sinhalese majority and Tamil and Muslim minorities.

In the midst of war, a generation of Sri Lanka's Tamil children has been left orphaned or homeless, refugees in their own country, often caught between two armies. Those who survive the brutality around them bear deep emotional wounds, trauma that the people of Sri Lanka and those involved in the peace process have been slow to address.

Since 1985, the LTTE has maintained a Women's Front—female fighters who are also sometimes called the "Liberation Birds." Today, these young girls form the core element of the Tigers' forces and have gained an international reputation as among the toughest, most committed warriors in the world. Most of the girls are trained for suicide bombing missions. In any given attack, half of the guerillas are women armed with rifles, grenades, or bombs. Once they have undergone ruthless physical and mental training, a closing ceremony takes place: Each girl is given a cyanide capsule to wear on a string around her neck. If captured, she must swallow it.

In 1987 the first female Tiger, Malathy, was killed in combat and would become a martyr to the cause. Within a month the LTTE declared war on the Indian peace-keeping force stationed on the Jaffna Peninsula. During that additional military engagement, the Tigers needed to boost their fighting ranks. For the first time, traditionally protected groups like women and children were forced to serve.

While the psycho-social impacts of the conflict have affected the entire child population, it has taken the heaviest toll on the approximately nine hundred thousand children living in the conflict-ridden areas in the north and east. A whole generation of children there knows nothing but war. Apart from the day-to-day stresses of coping in an uncertain and violent environment, children in this region have to bear an added trauma of being forced into direct military combat by the LTTE guerillas. The destruction of physical and social infrastructure, the irregular functioning of schools, and poor access to schooling for internally displaced children all mean that a large population of these children are not attending school.

"People are [now] fighting [against] the oppression of the Tamil people, but looking back, the struggle started in 1956," explained Joseph Parajashingham, a Tamil M.P. (member of parliament), at his office in Batticaloa one late-fall afternoon. I was joined by a photographer from New York. The office of the bespectacled, patient M.P. felt like a comfortable living room. Outside, a small crowd of village residents waited in a cramped reception area, bringing a variety of personal and community concerns.

"[That] year, the Prime Minister passed a law that put another language other than Tamil as the official language," he continued. "Tamil has been spoken for hundreds of years. This is where the ethnic problem began. The movement at first was a peaceful, passive Gandhian struggle, but youths involved with other groups took to arms because nothing was getting done. [By] 1983, the armed struggle was in full force."

Parajashingham had been a member of parliament for about ten years when we met in late 1999. His party, the moderate Tamil United Liberation Front, had been in existence since 1976. "The consequences of this war have been a complete oppression of the Tamil population," he said. "Over the last fifteen years, the war has had the largest number of casualties" since the Sinhalese-Tamil clashes started. "There have been numerous human rights violations, with many people having disappeared. The people responsible are the Sri Lankan security forces.

"There are two ways of going about things," he continued. "There is the passive democratic way, and then there is the armed struggle. The guerilla groups take up the two positions because they feel they have to adapt in their struggle. The suicide bombing was a concept that was introduced by the LTTE. The suicide bombers are usually youths or girls who are trying to be freedom fighters. They are not being paid anything, but they are doing it for a cause." Shifting in his seat, Parajashingham leaned forward and looked at me intently when I asked him if the Tigers were terrorists. In carefully measured words, he said, "I do not feel what they are doing is terrorism because they are fighting a war. No Tamil person would call the government 'terrorists.' The Tamil people and the LTTE are connected because they are both members of the Tamil community, not separate. Once the war ends, the Tamil people will stand by the LTTE."

Amnesty International and other international human rights groups alleged that the LTTE had been recruiting children as young as eleven for its fighting formations known as the "Baby Brigade." An attack of army camps in Weli Oya in 1995, where several of the LTTE casualties were children; a 1998 Mankulam attack, where twenty-six LTTE child combatants (boys and girls) surrendered to the army; and the October 1999 clashes between Security Forces and the LTTE, in which forty-nine children (mostly girls) ages eleven to fifteen were killed all support that finding. During the 1998 Sri Lankan visit of Olara Otunnu, UN Special Representative on Children in Armed Conflict, the LTTE promised that it would abide by the UN Convention on the Rights of the Child. However, the UN representative later admitted in a newspaper interview that the LTTE is one of the rebel groups that has failed to honor its commitment. Reports of both the University Teachers for Human Rights (an underground Tamil organization in Jaffna) as well as Amnesty International confirmed the prevalence of strong pressure on school children to join the LTTE cadres.

According to child protection experts in Sri Lanka, young recruits are trained for up to four months by the LTTE. Along with the weapons and explosives training is a heavy campaign of indoctrination. Propagandistic literature and flashy combat videos filmed by the Tigers provide the core of the recruits' daily diet. With a strict military code that includes respect for women fighters, the LTTE vehemently forbids sexual relations between recruits. A sexual assault or rape can mean a death sentence for the offender.

"In 1993, only 30 percent of the LTTE's casualties were [female]," said Rajan Hoole, a leader of the University Teachers for Human Rights (UTHR). "Today more than 60 percent are women." Hoole agreed to meet with me at a small guesthouse in Colombo, the Sri Lankan capital. Our meeting was arranged through a third party who would only tell me the place and time. UTHR is a target for both the Tamil Tigers and the Sri Lankan government because of its international criticism and documentation of human rights abuses. The use of girls as soldiers by the Tigers has been one of the organization's most highlighted issues.

"Traditionally, Tamil women were dependent on their male counterparts," continues Hoole. "After the war for Eelam started, men moved away or joined the struggle and died. You find instances where someone whose husband has been killed by the LTTE ends up taking work for them.

"It is possible to give the picture that this is just an insurgency like any other country, but that doesn't take into account the uniqueness of the LTTE. The use of suicide bombers is political bankruptcy. Because of the real military strength [against them], they had to resort to using sensational acts."

During my first trip to Sri Lanka on the eve of the millennium, in December 1999, I witnessed some of these "sensational acts." I was at the official residence one sultry afternoon as Sri Lankan President Chandrika Kumaratunga's chauffeured car pulled up to the entrance after passing through the tall iron gates. A young Tamil woman who'd been employed by the official staff for a short period moved toward the president carrying a purse with a false bottom. The bag held enough explosives to kill her and two dozen people standing nearby. Miraculously, Kumaratunga managed to exit from a different door, allowing the vehicle to absorb much of the blast, although she did suffer severe scars and lost an eye. On that same visit I watched as two other high-level leaders, a politician and a cabinet minister, were assassinated by female Tamil Tigers.

ASKING THE CHILDREN

Not unlike Rwanda and many other nations where children are combatants and victims of war, there has been a dearth of psycho-social assistance for and research about Sri Lankan youth. I realized early in this journey that, although not every child who survives war has post-traumatic stress or phsysical scars, most need help reentering society and moving past their combat experiences.

One evening, leaving my photographer to rest at the guesthouse in Colombo, I rode a tri-shaw taxi to a quiet suburb to visit with one of the preeminent authorities on the mental health of child soldiers and war-affected children in the world. For an hour or so, we sat in the dimly lit sitting room of Harendra de Silva's home as his family moved around preparing dinner in the kitchen behind us. De Silva is a professor of pediatrics at the University of Kelaniya in the inner city of Tyrannia near Colombo and the chair of the Child Protection Agency of Sri Lanka. His main focus is child abuse. The official definition of child abuse in Sri Lanka is "an act or omission by an adult or caregiver which leads to actual or potential damage of a child." It hardly seems necessary to have to prove that children involved in a country's armed conflicts experience a form of abuse, but that has been his task. In 1995, he conducted a landmark study in Sri Lanka of ex-combatants. "One of the problems I saw is their reasons for joining. There's a fear of being taken away by government forces. Some join for economic reasons, and others because they are made to wear a uniform and given a gun, which makes them feel secure."

Many people have examined the psychological aspects of children at war, but de Silva was the first to deal with child abuse from the point of view of a child, not of the political situation. In 1995 he administered a questionnaire to nineteen children in a rehabilitation camp who claimed to be ex-combatants.

"Child soldiers in Sri Lanka are more involved in more aspects of making mines, manufacturing bombs, and making children commit suicide, which is different from the world," he pointed out. "Committing suicide is an attack on a child, 'suicide-by-proxy.' The child is made to do this by a process of persuasion and can't understand what is going on."

De Silva's study was done with former child soldiers who were then in government-run centers. There are two centers for boy soldiers and one for girls. His study was done at the boys' centers. Some of the boys had had father figures at the guerillas' camp, and they'd felt secure in the group. When he asked their reasons for joining, a common answer was the fear of being taken away by government forces. A child soldier with a uniform and a weapon feels safer than one in fear of abduction. Another common answer was that it was heroic to be a freedom fighter, or simply that they'd joined for economic reasons.

"In the future, when the time of peace comes, you are going to have a large number of traumatized people," noted de Silva. "Everybody will have to be ready to face the problems of these traumatized people. The country is not prepared to deal with this. Right now, there are six clinical psychologists for the entire country and twenty psychiatrists. We don't have the people or resources to help [everyone]."

On my first visit to Sri Lanka, I had the opportunity to visit one of the rehabilitation camps where Dr. de Silva had conducted his research. The Bandarawela Bindunawarena Camp was located in the foothills of north-central Sri Lanka in an overwhelmingly Sinhalese, rural community. The camp was under the jurisdiction of the government's Ministry of Youth Affairs. No one was armed—not even the captain, a burly, jovial man who had been in charge of the center for about five years. Seventy-five males ranging in age from thirteen to thirty-five years old would live there until the authorities decided they had been "rehabilitated" and were committed to an allegiance to the Sri Lankan government—theoretically, one year. During that time they would receive psychological counseling and vocational training, language classes in Hindu, Tamil, and English, religious services for those who were Hindu or Christian, and recreational activities such as soccer and volleyball.

"The families really do not visit the trainees at the camp," explained the director, who requested that his name not be used. "After the trainee is finished with the camp, they return home. Sometimes trainees come back to visit, as the staff has a good cooperation with them. There are twenty-four staff members, and the most number of [inmates] at one time is 128. All are former members of the LTTE. They go to jail and then to the rehabilitation center. The staff here is both Sinhalese and Tamil, but Tamil is the language we use in working with them."

One of the inmates I met had a typical story among the former fighters and had been at the camp only a short time. Nixon, twenty-four years old, had joined the Tigers when he was fourteen. "The LTTE gave me three months' physical training," he told me. "After eighteen months, I lost my leg while fighting. I became a member because I had nothing else to do. They did not pay me. The day I lost my leg, [they] lost twenty people. I was in the hospital for some time, and then they asked me to work in the office. I came here to the center because I surrendered. I want to study computers and advanced systems and also live in a peaceful place."

The youngest person at the rehabilitation camp was Darmalingham, who was thirteen. He had fought with the Tigers for only a month. The LTTE had come to his home and forced him to go with them. While we spoke, he rolled up his sleeve to show me a bullet hole in his arm.

"I was caught by the police," he explained. "I didn't like to fight, and escaped with a fifteen-year-old. I'm afraid the LTTE will take me," he said, sounding as if he were repeating the statement by rote. He did write his sister and younger brother regularly, and up to that point, they had managed to stay safe from the fighting and recruitment by the Tigers.

IDA

The need for security plays a big factor in the participation of women in the Tamil Tigers. As with Ida Carmelita's situation, being a member of the LTTE can be a useful deterrent against sexual assault or exploitation at the hands of the government forces, paramilitary groups, or even civilian neighbors. If a woman is a civilian or decides to leave her combat status behind, as Ida did, the risks of gender-based exploitation are high. In the summer of 2000, Amnesty International released an alert recognizing the widespread incidence of sexual abuse directed against Tamil women. In particular, Tamil women taken into official custody have been vulnerable to torture and sexual abuse at the hands of police and military soldiers. "Because it's a war zone, human rights abuses are expected," says Radhika Coomaraswamy, the UN Special Rapporteur on Violence against Women, who is based in Colombo. "The judiciary is very cautious when these cases arise, and the women feel they have no recourse."

During the four years Ida spent in the field for the Tamil Tigers, she lived with the constant fear of death and the chaotic horror of combat. Her older brother Napoleon, who'd joined the guerillas before Ida, left in disillusionment in 1997. "I took him to the Thallady army camp and surrendered him to the brigadier," explained their mother, Sebastiana. He'd had to turn himself in to the police and was jailed, but eventually he was allowed to return to Mannar to visit Sebastiana and the rest of the family. He convinced Ida to get out two years later.

Before she could go home, though, the Tigers made her undergo a year of "punishment," akin to forced labor. "Ida sent me a letter saying she wanted to leave, and I took the letter to the intelligence commander," Sebastiana continued. "'I am going to bring my child, and you have to help me.' He told me, 'She can come, and we will offer her protection.'" Ida left the LTTE in Puthukkudiyiruppu and then traveled to Adampan, where Sebastiana went to meet her. The army came at 10:30 in the morning and took her straight to the intelligence camp. Ida made an official statement and was allowed to return home with her mother that afternoon.

"The intelligence office gave me a letter and said, 'If anyone comes, show them the letter and don't worry,'" recalled Sebastiana. It was June 19, 1999, and Ida Carmelita had served as a guerilla soldier for the Tamil Tigers for slightly more than three years.

She never talked about her experiences as a Tiger with her mother. The young combat veteran wanted a new life and hoped to finish the schooling that had been interrupted years before in India. But the fate of war intervened again to alter Ida's life.

Sebastiana and I met face-to-face five months after Ida had returned home. Traveling by bus and car north from Colombo, my photographer and I arrived in Mannar in late December 1999. A Catholic priest whose name I'd been given met with us at his church and arranged a meeting with Sebastiana at her family's home, a short distance from the ocean. It was cool and slightly overcast as we walked through deserted residential side streets to an enclave of houses situated in jagged rows. A small crowd of neighbors and curious onlookers watched us enter the house, mostly transfixed by our appearance. En route to the house, the priest had given us a brief background on Sebastiana's family and what had happened to Ida.

Sebastiana was a stout woman with a sad but gentle demeanor. She seemed happy that my photographer and I were there, as foreigners expressing interest in what she had to say. We stood in the front area of her sparse two- room house. I strained to hear her soft voice speaking through shadows. We were not alone—three bystanders hovered as she recounted the story—but hers were the only voice and figure I noticed. The walls were dingy, and the cement floor was highly polished. A large red stain extended out beyond our feet. No amount of scrubbing had been able to remove the constant reminder of a tragic night months before.

There were no lights on in the room, and consequently, everyone present cast long shadows across the walls. A bird cawed somewhere outside and our voices echoed in the space, making the room feel absolutely hollow. The fifty-six-year-old woman was either in tears or right on the verge of them the entire time we spoke. She told me that in the early morning of July 12, 1999, she was home along with Ida, two grandchildren by her daughter Snekalatha, her son Hitlar, his son Anthony, and a family acquaintance, Mr. Kanthan. A shopkeeper named Kesavan Rajah who ran a vegetable store across the street knocked on the door looking for Ida. When Sebastiana opened it, five masked men knocked him down and barged in.

Raju would later testify that he recognized the men as customers in his shop who were soldiers from the Pallimunai Army Camp nearby.

"Someone knocked on the door of my shop," he recalled. "When I opened, I saw two people. Two others were hiding nearby, but I could not identify them. They took me to Ida's house and wanted me to wake her up. When I knocked on the door, Ida's mother came. One of them hit me on my face, and I fell down. Then they took off my sarong and tied my hands and feet. They went into the house and pulled out everyone inside, but Ida was not among them. I was lying down and saw what was happening. They took me inside the house, and I found Ida was inside a room. [Later], we found Ida lying in a pool of blood, half-naked."

Sebastiana described that night as if it had occurred the day before. "When I heard Raju's voice, I opened the door and found two armed men with their faces covered with a cloth below their eyes. They were wearing trousers, a banian [tank top], gloves on their hands, and holsters. I did not see Raju, as it was very dark. Someone asked me where my son Napoleon was," she said. "I said, 'He has gone to Colombo.' I didn't know who the men with the shopkeeper were, so I asked. They said they were from the 'movement.' When I said that my son was not here, they slapped me on my face.

"From outside I could see one of them pulling off the sheet with which my daughter Ida was covering herself. He asked me who it was and I replied that it was my daughter. One of them pulled me into the courtyard, where I saw Raju seated on the ground. They pulled off the sarong being worn by him and blindfolded me with it. Then I heard them calling [everyone] to come out. My daughter began to cry out loud, and they told my son to tell her not to shout. He requested her not to shout and came with her outside. She came and sat by my side and buried her face in my lap, sobbing.

"After about two minutes, my blindfold was removed, and all were asked to get inside the house. We all went into the bigger room. They then called one by one the three males except Raju and put them into the other room and closed the door. Through fear I was also shouting, and they came and slapped me several times for shouting.

"Then they pulled me by my hair to the courtyard, where I saw three more armed men. They took a sarong from our fence and gagged me with it, twisted my hands and tied them behind me, then pushed me onto the ground, and two men pressed me down with their feet. First, the two men who came earlier went inside the house, and after about three minutes, the other three too went inside. I then managed to sit up and then to stand. Thinking of diverting their attention to myself and off the children, I ran fast outside our compound and along the road. My hands got loosened by that time, and I pulled out the gag from my mouth. I went to the house of a relative and asked for a lantern. While there, we heard one gunshot first and then five to six more afterwards.

"I ran to the police station and told them what had happened and about the gunshots and appealed to them to come to our help. They replied, 'We cannot come now, and you need to go home.' But I sat for about two hours in front of the police station. I went to another relative's house, and told them that I would stay with them till dawn. At about 6 AM, I requested them to go and find out what had happened. Seeman Jovan went to our home and returned and informed us that my daughter had been shot and killed. I then [went] home and found many people already gathered there."

When Sebastiana went inside, she discovered a sight that nearly broke her. "Ida had been covered with a bedsheet by my son and nephew. She was face up on the front living room floor. Her eyes were still open." It was the same room in which we now sat.

"I have lost all faith in human beings," Sebastiana said flatly. "People often say God had cursed my family. But I cannot forsake him. For a widow like me, who is the protector? Unless the Lord guards the household, guarding a house is in vain. No army or group of people can protect helpless people like us. I have seen too much suffering. Three children killed in front of my eyes."

Nine days after her death, Ida's body and half a dozen weapons that had been retrieved from the scene of the murder were examined in

Colombo. She'd been repeatedly raped, shot in the genitals, and mutilated. A total of eighteen bodily injuries had been inflicted from guns or
human bites.

"I know Ida grabbed the guns; she tried to fight," Sebastiana said.
"One of her fingers was shot off so that's what I surmise. Ida had military
training. She would have pulled at their guns."

———————

The Bishop of Mannar, Dr. Rayappu Joseph, wrote President Chan-
drinka Kumaratunga in October 1999 to push forward as quickly as possible on the investigation and trial of the case, but as of this writing, it has
not been resolved. Several days after I visited with Sebastiana, he received
me in his office. Until 2000, the Jaffna Peninsula in northern Sri Lanka
had been an off-limits LTTE stronghold. Bishop Joseph's predecessor
oversaw the church's activities there. One of his subordinates, a Father
Herbert, had also been killed recently. It was suspected a Muslim mob
had murdered him following his defense of a Tamil boy accused of a
crime.

Bishop Joseph was responsible for twenty-five parishes and fifty-one
priests in an area where 60 percent of the population was Catholic.
Though his sympathies likely leaned more to the side of the Tamil
Tigers, he was seen as a trusted intermediary by both the government and
the rebels.

"Both of these parties, they accept us as people who can be trusted,
and it seems we have played a neutral role," he explained to me over tea.
"Tamil people in general, they consider the LTTE as liberation fighters.
I don't think the people consider them as terrorists. There are terrorist
activities, on both sides—government side and LTTE side—but this is
not liberation stuggle. Liberation struggle is different from terrorist
events. There is a lot of talk about children being used by the LTTE, but
I have never been able to see that. I always objected to that, and we al-

ways as a church stand against that, against the use of children for armed struggles."

In response to the death of Ida Carmelita, the bishop and his allies pressured the Presidential Secretariat in Colombo to lead the investigation, particularly in light of the local authorities' obvious cover-up of what happened. Ida's body was exhumed and taken to Colombo where the graphic brutality of her death was revealed. The bishop had also been writing to newspapers about the case and inviting human rights organizations to advocate for a true investigation. A petition had been signed by six thousand women and girls in Mannar to pressure the president to order a special investigation into Ida's death.

"There has not been any significant response because the armed forces are involved in this," Bishop Joseph told me. "This is the normal situation here. We, as Tamils, can be treated as dirt, and nobody is there to question us unless people get interested. This group who murdered [Ida] had already publicly done six similar murders on this island. This is not a 'different' murder. This is a human being who had a legal right to live in this country. Just because she had been in the Tigers doesn't mean she has less of a right to live here. She came and surrendered herself legally, and had been accepted. From August 1998 to December 1998, we had about thirty-seven cases like this in this area. And no cases taken, no culprits brought to the law. We always carry the light of hope in this conflict that's a dark situation."

A TAMIL CAMP

Having met Ida's mother and family, talked to Dr. de Silva, and visited a camp for former child soldiers, I was anxious to meet the Tigers myself. Arranging it required an unbelievable amount of legwork and meetings with Tamil representatives in New York and London. Two years after that first visit and a month after the September 11 attacks, I returned alone to Sri Lanka with the sole intent of meeting with the Tigers. Arguably, I should have spent more time talking with victims and government representatives for their take on the Tigers. But I felt I needed to see them through Tamil eyes.

Several weeks into my trip, it had begun to look like things were falling apart again. A plan would be made with someone representing the Tigers, and a date would be set for a meeting. Then, arrangements inevitably became scuttled, and I would start the process all over again. Following a motorcycle crash in which I broke several toes and after experiencing a free-falling depression from loneliness and the inability to make any progress in my mission, I received word that I would finally be taken to meet the Tigers in northeast Sri Lanka. My companion would be a guide sent by the Tigers to lead me to my final destination, an LTTE camp. The route would go through Muthur, a poor rural community. To get there, I had to take a hair-raising boat ride across an extremely choppy stretch of the Indian Ocean, packed in with about forty other passengers on a rickety wooden boat.

That was only the beginning of a long day of travel to reach the Tigers. Once in Muthur, I hitched a ride on the back of a too-small motorbike and rode through a military checkpoint separating the government-controlled territory from the "uncleared" or Tiger-held region. About a mile past the checkpoint, I got off and walked five miles under a scorching sun without water. My companion and I were more than a little dazed by the time we reached a small lagoon where a wizened Tamil man sat waiting in a dugout canoe. He would take me across the lagoon first.

I gingerly squeezed myself into the questionable raft, and we inched across the still water. There were no signs or visible markings, but somehow I knew we were under the Tigers' authority at that point. There was no road or trail leading up from the lagoon, more like pockmarked scoops of earth and muddy gashes from villagers' walking back and forth to the lagoon or trying to ride bicycles and motorbikes.

Again, my companion and I walked a long distance, dragging from the heat and dehydration. Ninety minutes later, after passing a series of lean-tos, flimsy huts, and mud-brick houses, we reached a huge well from which a young girl was pulling up water in a bucket to wash clothes.

We enthusiastically quenched our thirst and drenched our sticky clothing, then rested before going on to meet Rubin, the local LTTE political commander. Finally, I would meet the Tigers and see firsthand this hardened force that inspired respect and fear around the world. We met Rubin in a campus-like vocational school. He turned out to be a slightly built man with a thick moustache, but his soft-spoken manner masked what I felt was a determined personality. Over the course of several hours that first afternoon in Tiger-controlled territory, we spoke at length about the mission of the LTTE and its use of girls and suicide bombers.

"The LTTE succeeds because this is the people's base movement, movement with the people's support," he continued. "It is not 'suicide bombing.' From our point of view, we consider it a 'life weapon,' not suicide. Becoming a Tiger is a personal choice. In the course of participating in the struggle, some militants prefer to commit themselves to be a member of the Tigers. I feel that this is more constructive and productive in terms of commitment, but my leader decides whether that person is capable, suitable, or preferable to be a member of the Tigers. This is the manifestation of the highly motivated commitment to sacrifice their life for the liberation of Tamil Eelam."

The Muthur district was well-maintained and comparatively prosperous. Electrical lines ran throughout the community, the dirt roads were level and well-packed, and the majority of the homes were brick and concrete. The most stunning sight was the Tiger cadre themselves. Everywhere I turned were wiry, intense-looking young women armed with Kalashnikov rifles. As I was told they would be, all of the female recruits had their long dark hair braided and wrapped into a bun on the back of their heads.

They all wore the same clothing: checkered blue shirts, black pants, flip-flop sandals, and thin glass-encased cyanide capsules around their necks. Even their physical builds were similar—most were short in stature, making it difficult to gauge their ages. Whenever I approached them with my camera or even a smile, all backed away warily. A few motivated by obvious curiosity followed me to see what I would do.

Although I knew that there were a number of female Tiger commanders, I didn't see any during the first of my two days there. The girl fighters stood outside the homes of people I assumed were commanders, as well as the school where Rubin and I met.

The following day was the start of Heroes Week, and there was an even greater number of female soldiers in the area. Every November, the LTTE mounts this annual event to memorialize the slain Tiger soldiers and express a public recommitment to continuing the struggle for another year. To recognize the occasion, the roadsides were lined with displays of yellow and orange ribbons. In an open field near the vocational school, a huge tent had been erected with ribbons and militaristic banners.

At the entrance to the area, a sign in Tamil language read, "Eternally, your remembrance is deep in our heart." From early in the morning, soldiers started going in and out of the tent. Inside along the walls were newspaper pictures, snapshots, and even drawings of all the LTTE soldiers who'd been killed from that area. Many but not all of the fallen were females.

At the far wall in the center, one of the most prominent displays of flowers stood next to a photograph of Second Lieutenant Malathy, the first female LTTE soldier to be killed.

"We are prepared to fight until liberation is achieved," said Rubin. "Our goal is Tamil Eelam, an independent state."

Not all Tamils believe war is the only route, particularly for children. In Batticaloa, on the northeastern coast, the Butterfly Garden has been an oasis of reconciliation for Tamil, Muslim, and Sinhalese children over the last decade. It was created by a Tamil Catholic priest known as Father Paul. We spoke on a number of occasions during my trips to the island, and despite the escalating violence in those times, he remained optimistic.

"This is definitely an important point to be emphasized, that these children have lost their childhood experience completely," he explained. "Practically all these children have lost their real playfulness and that excitement and enthusiasm, because this whole environment is a kind of traumatizing experience for these children. All the playgrounds and all the play activity centers have been robbed from them by the adult world, who is just engaged in their war that is just not sensible and doesn't have any meaning.

"What could really heal these youth is the family environment, but the family environment is completely destroyed," he continued. "So now what do they do? They go through this experience, and I feel that there is a kind of mechanism, psychic mechanism within the child, where I think some of these children become very resilient. And there is a self-healing process that is taking place it looks like, even though such traumatizations have occurred. In their hearts, they want love, peace, and to live together."

PAINFUL JOURNEYS

For many families and youth in Sri Lanka, escaping the war does not guarantee happiness or justice. Following our visit to the Bandarawela Rehabilitation camp for former boy soldiers of the LTTE, my photographer and I had had high hopes and optimism for the youth we had encountered. Their intelligence and sincere passion for improving their lives and existing as normal, everyday civilians left an impression. Unfortunately, the dreams many of them had expressed to us formally and informally did not come to fruition.

On the morning of October 27, 2000, approximately a thousand attackers laid siege to the camp with knives, axes, and blunt weapons, while many of the young men were asleep or just waking up. More than two dozen of them died, and nearly the same number were left severely injured. After tearing the camp apart, the attackers set fire to it, burning wounded residents alive. With no weapons on site, there was little hope of repelling the attack. The Bandarawela police asked for backup from army soldiers at the nearby Diyathalawe Army Camp, but by the time troops arrived, the center had been completely destroyed, bodies had been burned beyond recognition, and the perpetrators had long since fled.

The next day, hundreds of villagers from Bandarawela were taken to the police station for their alleged roles in the attack, including women and the elderly. Faced with barely contained resistance, the police offered to release most of the assembled group if fifty of them would volunteer to confess and be arrested for the assault. Infuriated, the townspeople resisted, and everyone was released.

Eventually, a government investigation into the incident revealed that racist posters against Tamil Sri Lankans had been put up shortly before the attack. Businessmen in Bandarawela had encouraged popular dissent against Tamils, especially those who were at the rehabilitation center. Shortly before the October 27 massacre, the former child soldiers at the camp managed to carry out a hunger strike and briefly take two employees hostage. They were protesting what they saw as a too-long internment, even appealing to the International Committee of the Red Cross for protection.

The truth was that the people living in the local community near the camp had gotten along fine with the youth there, in contrast to the police version. In fact, many former child soldiers had done community work helping to repair roads, clear Buddhist temples of refuse, and draw water from the camp well.[1]

In 2004, five people with no direct ties to the camp or local community were given the death penalty for the twenty-seven people who died during the camp attack, but the sentences were quickly commuted to twenty-three years' imprisonment. Prior to that, twenty-three people, including a police officer and the director of the camp, whom I'd interviewed, were acquitted of having taken part in the massacre. The Sri Lankan Human Rights Commission said that the police were guilty of "grave dereliction of duty." They'd been charged with taking part in the killings and with doing nothing to prevent the villagers from entering the detention camp.

———

For Sebastiana Figerardo, justice still had not come five years after her daughter Ida's rape and murder at the hands of army soldiers. The two grandchildren who had witnessed Ida's ordeal were afraid to say anything. But still the family began to receive death threats from the police. A short time after I met Sebastiana, she fled to the Tamil Nadu state of India, along with her grandchildren, their parents, and her brother. One of Ida's brothers was arrested on suspicion of terrorist activities there and detained for three years in a special camp, but with the help of the United Nations High Commissioner for Refugees, they all managed to return to Sri Lanka in January 2004. The house where Sebastiana raised her seven children, and where three of them had died, was no longer there. They were living outside of Mannar when the December 2004 tsunami wracked the island nation. Their community was among the most devastated. Sebastiana had expressed hopes of getting her entire family away from Sri Lanka, as far away from the war as possible.

"I expect some justice to be done for my daughter," she said. "At the same time, I feel like nothing like this should happen to other people like my daughter. I believe in God. God will give justice, and eventually the government will bring justice to me. I'm not afraid, I'm not afraid if I die today. When God calls me, I'll be ready to go. If they want to kill me, they don't need to come here and rape my child. God gives me the strength to bear all this. The last thing Ida said to me was that she felt that ever since she left the Tigers, she would ultimately die. Before they dragged her into the house, she'd put her head in my lap and said, 'I'm afraid.' Ida had told me she would stay with me until I died. Now I only have her identity card to remember her."

NOTES

1. U.S. State Department, "Country Reports on Human Rights Practices, 2000," Bureau of Democracy, Human Rights, and Labor, 2001, p. 3.

4

Deliver Us from Evil: Faith and the Children's War in Northern Uganda

I HAD IMAGINED MY FIRST FIREFIGHT would somehow be a proud tale to be recounted over and over for friends and family. When it did unfold, on an eerily quiet road between the towns of Gulu and Kitgum in northern Uganda during the early spring of 1999, the experience was instead something I tried to bury and forget, rarely mentioning it to anyone. It happened the day before I was scheduled to leave the country and return home. I'd been there for a month, seeking to learn about one of the least known, most bizarre conflicts in the world.

After spending a week or so in the community of Gulu, I decided to make a short visit to the nearby village of Kitgum. Relief workers and Gulu citizens had warned me not to go by road, even though the trip could be made in an afternoon. Carelessly ignoring the warnings, I arranged for an SUV to take me and an assistant from Gulu just after dawn one morning. A mini dust storm kicked up around us as our obviously nervous driver sped along the narrow road, passing overloaded passenger minivans and pedestrians in a hazy blur.

I was going to Kitgum in order to see an Anglican bishop, as well as visit child-oriented humanitarian programs. About halfway there, we fell in line behind an International Committee of the Red Cross vehicle. Our driver relaxed behind the wheel, and I settled back to take a nap. My colleague and translator, a young Ugandan student I had met through a member of parliament who had befriended me, sat quietly in the backseat, staring out the window.

When the gunfire erupted, my eyes flew open, and I saw the Red Cross truck just ahead of us, now stopped and taking shots from both sides of the narrow road. I could make out raggedly dressed figures emerging from the bush and firing automatic weapons. Our driver threw the vehicle into reverse and floored the accelerator. The Red Cross driver also went into reverse but at a much slower speed. A minivan filled with commuters going from Gulu to Kitgum was stopped on the side of the road.

"Ambush!" screamed my driver. My friend in the backseat stared through the windshield, eyes wide with fear. I was scared, too, but more exhilarated than anything, wanting to get into the action somehow.

We'd passed a Ugandan army sentry post half a mile back. Coming over a high bend in the road, we approached it again. The driver of my truck got out to tell the assembled soldiers what was happening, as we listened to the sporadic gunfire just over the hill. The youthful military men ran to the shooting, and I ran after them with my video camera.

Initially there was only a fifty-yard gap between me and the army squad as I gave chase. One arm furiously pumped and wiped the tide of sweat coming from my face, while the other tried to point the camera in the general direction of the soldiers ahead. The distance between us quickly grew to seventy-five yards, then a hundred. By the time I reached the top of the hill, they were no longer in sight. Hunched over and gasping for breath, I cursed myself for being so out of shape.

I made the fateful decision to follow the sound of the soldiers into the bush, where they were exchanging automatic weapons fire with the rebels who'd ambushed the road. The tall grass prevented me from seeing who was who, but I could hear the army squad leader calling out orders in one area and unintelligible conversation in another. Within five minutes I realized I was lost between the two sides, in the middle of a steady firefight. Now, moving low and hunched over, I felt scared—not of being accidentally shot, but of being captured by the ambushers.

The next hour seemed like a day as I tried to get as far away from the shooting as I could, running in the opposite direction of the gunfire. Finally slowing down for breath and in the hope of finding water, I came across a farmer carrying a hoe and a sack over one shoulder. From about twenty yards away we spotted each other. I waved and held up my video camera so that he could see I was unarmed. Instead of waving me over, he moved quickly away from me.

Eventually I began looping back in what I thought was the direction of the main road. Stumbling onto it near the place where the army squad was questioning passengers of the minivan, I sat down, grinning from ear to ear in relief. I hadn't seen who it was that had attacked, killing the passenger in the Red Cross vehicle and critically wounding its driver. But I knew who they were: members of the Lord's Resistance Army. The LRA was widely known and feared in Uganda as the guerilla fighting force of a man named Joseph Kony.

During the trips I made to Uganda in 1999 and 2000, I never met face to face with Kony, but I had traveled there to learn about him and the horror he wrought on this East African nation. A towering figure wearing aviator sunglasses and with a full head of beaded hair, Kony claimed to be *lakwena*, which means "messenger" in the Acholi language. After hearing the stories of what he had done and meeting his victims, I wondered who he thought sent him to bring a message of destruction and fear. From his base in southern Sudan, he waged a campaign of intimidation and terror against civilians of the Acholi ethnic group—of which he was a member—and the government of Ugandan president Yoweri K. Museveni.

On his orders, hundreds of international relief convoys were attacked and raided for supplies. Rural towns fell under siege, during which scores of people were burned alive or hacked to pieces with machetes and panga sticks. Countless tales emerged of suspected informers having their lips or ears severed. He forbade bicycle riding, and anyone caught atop one had their feet amputated. The Lord's Resistance Army was not comprised of disgruntled political opponents returning from exile or secessionists hoping for autonomy. The bulk of foot soldiers exacting Joseph Kony's apocalyptic vision were children. From boarding schools, churches, and isolated farms he took upward of ten thousand girls and boys since the LRA started fighting in 1986. Typically in the process he murdered their families and neighbors or forced the youths to do it.

As a result of the war he instigated with the Ugandan government, many innocent civilian bystanders suffered cruelly. For their protection thousands were moved into transit camps throughout upper Uganda, living scarce existences in tent communities. Many more children walked to these communities from remote villages every night for shelter and the semblance of security in hospital compounds or heavily populated locations. They were "night commuters" or "daytrippers" seeking safety from abduction by Kony and the Lord's Resistance Army.

Children taken by Joseph Kony faced one of four fates: they became foot soldiers in his personal insurgency; they became porters who carried supplies or farming equipment; they were sold to neighboring Sudanese for arms and supplies; or they were murdered as an example, to toughen up other abductees. When I first traveled to Uganda, somewhere around five thousand had returned home, but thousands more were dead or missing. The LRA was not the only insurgency group operating in Uganda, but it was certainly the largest and most feared. At the beginning of my journey a local journalist had suggested to me, "To understand Kony, you must understand him from the level he operates. Sometimes, you will think the Devil himself has fled Hell and is living in northern Uganda."

Mention Uganda to most people outside the African continent, and images of Idi Amin's bloody eight-year reign are conjured. First explored by European and Arab traders in the mid-1800s, Uganda was formally incorporated into the British Empire in 1890. British Prime Minister Winston Churchill nicknamed it the "Pearl of Africa." The country finally became independent on October 9, 1962. Twice the size of the state of Pennsylvania, it is bordered by five countries, only two of which are at peace. Over a dozen ethnic groups live in Uganda, with none having a sizable majority. The Acholis, of which Joseph Kony was a member, comprised only 4 percent of the population of seven million.

Nine years after independence, army general Idi Amin overthrew the government of Milton Obote and throughout the 1970s led the country with a notoriously cruel hand, expelling thousands of Indian residents and murdering political dissidents and civilians. In 1979, Tanzanian soldiers allied with the Uganda National Liberation Army succeeded in ousting Amin and marched into the capital, Kampala. After a succession of short-lived regimes, Yoweri Museveni took over in 1986 and has been president ever since.

"A culture of violence has been engrained in the society," Livingstone Sewanyana, executive director of the Foundation for Human Rights Initiative, explained to me one afternoon at his office in Kampala. "People are used to holding power by the gun. It's now to the extent that the gun is being used by children. We saw the first use of children as soldiers by Museveni. When he and his allies were fighting, there was a strong outcry against the use of children." An estimated three thousand children under the age of fifteen fought with Museveni in his struggle to topple the second presidency of Milton Obote. Over four and a half years, his forces cared for abandoned children, but increasing numbers of school-aged children were also absorbed into the ranks.

"What we see is a common pattern in that Kony has resorted to the abduction of children," continued Sewanyana. "The problem with children using guns is that they don't discriminate. Because of our politics in this country, the issue of abducted children and child combatants hasn't resonated. Conflicts tend to gain a degree of sympathy in the areas where they are occurring, [and] because the south has historically been subservient to the north, militarily, there's the [attitude] that 'now it's [their] time.'"

THE MAKING OF A MONSTER

The only indisputable knowledge about Joseph Kony's life is the havoc he wreaked upon northern Uganda. Stories vary, but one of the more reliable accounts that I chose to pursue puts his birth around 1964 or 1965. Lakony Joseph Aringa was the eldest son of farmers from Odek in Omora County within the district of Gulu, a sparsely populated settlement whose primary source of income was agriculture. Kony's parents grew mainly cotton, but also maize, cassava, and sweet potatoes. The closest neighbors lived several miles away, but a trading center to buy goods and equipment was nearby.

Lakony means "I'm helping you" and is a fairly common name in Acholiland. Shortened to Kony, the name simply means "help." His mother gave him the name Aringa because she claimed that during her pregnancy with him, the father left for a period to another district, but eventually returned. *Aringa* means "he's run away from me."

The exact number of siblings is unclear because in Ugandan society it is quite common to take in the children of other relatives, who are called "brother" and "sister." Somewhere between five and ten children grew up in Joseph Kony's family. He was friendly to his siblings, but if they crossed him in any way, he often came down hard. His mother would gather the children around the fireplace at night to tell them stories and give each one advice about living a good life.

"[Kony] had compassion for people and was friendly," said one man who knew him in his youth. "He used to help in the community, what we call *alea*. If someone needed help to cultivate their land or build a grass-roof hut, he was in the front line." Described as an introvert, the young Kony didn't speak very much and was somewhat reserved, like his father. If confronted, he would usually resort to his fists rather than parrying verbally. People feared him because of his great height at an early age and his strength. He had friends, but not many.

Growing up, he never expressed any particular ambitions. The furthest he went in school was P6, which is the equivalent of seventh grade in the American school system. The school fees at the Anyau Primary School weren't high; it's just that Kony didn't want to go. He was teased by the other students because of his size, and the teachers gave him a hard time because he wasn't considered bright.

His father, who apparently had little influence over him, was a lay apostle in the Catholic church. His mother was Anglican. Young Joseph was an altar boy for several years, although he never showed any particular spiritual leaning. For two hours every Sunday morning he would meticulously press his robe. He stopped attending church when he was about fifteen or sixteen years old.

The uncles on his father's side were close to the family, and Joseph had an aunt, his mother's sister, whom he liked very much. She lived in a place called Anaka about fifty miles away, so he visited her only occasionally. Kony liked her mostly because she would praise him for being strong and handsome. She also told him to lead a good life and set a positive example in the village, maybe even become a chief. When he returned from trips to see her, his pockets would bulge with the money she'd given him from her private beer-making business.

There was a game the local children used to play at which Kony showed a great deal of skill. Gathering bunches of the wild reeds that sprouted in the area, the youths would shape crude wheels and then throw them. Using sticks shaped like spears, the aim of the game was to stop the wheel from rolling by piercing it. The first person to do so was the "killer." Another popular activity he was good at was hunting a small animal they called *anyeri*, which means "edible rat."

As a young teenager, Joseph committed an offense against another boy in the village that apparently brought him a great deal of embarrassment. One day a group of boys went out into the bush in search of wild fruits and berries to eat. Kony went along with his bow and arrow, shooting wild rabbits and *anyeri*. In the group was a boy with whom Kony had a serious rivalry. During the outing the boy climbed a tree and crawled to a branch that he claimed for himself, as it appeared to be the heaviest with fruit. Out of envy Kony shot him in the buttocks with the bow and arrow, sending him hurling to the ground. As punishment, Kony was taken to the *gumbullah*, or county chief, and caned in front of all the boys and many adults. The elders warned the other boys that when a person does such an act against another, it comes back to them.

Whenever a person in the community did something extremely admirable or disdained, a melody was composed relating to the incident.

Whenever Kony came around, the kids would hum the song and dance to it. He could only walk away in shame. He never spoke about it.

Not long after he dropped out of school, family and friends recognized how unruly he had become. His parents had refused to grant his wish to join the army. If he had done so without their blessing, the culture would have considered it an omen of bad things to come. Kony stopped listening to his mother. When told to do a chore such as cutting trees or tending goats, he would delegate the tasks to one of the other children, while he went to hang out at the trading center, returning late in the evening.

When Museveni came to power in 1986, disaffected Acholi in the military left its ranks and started a resistance force, the Ugandan People's Democratic Army (UPDA). The momentum of this movement fluctuated constantly in the face of demoralization and failure to gain ground. During this time a woman named Alice Auma arrived in the forefront of Acholi resistance. Some accounts establish a familial link between Alice and Joseph. Claiming to be a prophetess, she called herself Alice Lakwena and established a movement inspired by the Holy Spirit of God. Her belief was that the Acholi could succeed in defeating Museveni's government by casting off the witchcraft and spiritualism embedded in their culture.

Guided by the Holy Spirit force, Alice urged potential followers to heed twenty "precautions" or commandments with regard to combat, such as rubbing their bodies with shea nut oil as a defense against an enemy's bullets, never taking cover or retreating in the face of battle, and never killing snakes or bees.

Support of Alice Lakwena's Holy Spirit Mobile Force grew among the Acholi, particularly the youth. In the meantime Kony was thought to have become possessed by spirits. Instead of the typical route of calling in a witch doctor for a cure, he became a spiritual figure, or medium. To the surprise of many, Lakwena scored several key victories on the battlefield against the government's forces and began a march toward Kampala, south of Gulu and Acholiland. Joseph Kony seized upon this opportunity to recruit UPDA and Holy Spirit remnants for his own movement. In 1997, when Lakwena was defeated in Jinja, an hour away from Kampala, and fled to Kenya, Kony became leader of the Holy Spirit Mobile Force II, which eventually became the Lord's Resistance Army. I visited Lakwena and the remnants of her followers at Dadoob refugee camp in northern Kenya. Overseen by the United Nations High Commissioner for Refugees (UNHCR), the camp was desolate and situated in a dry, dusty region. The small enclave in which Lakwena resided numbered less than a hundred, consisting mostly of small families.

Just getting to the camp was an adventure. I had to take an early morning flight on a chartered plane to northern Kenya. Arriving at a United Nations compound, I then faced an hour's drive by 4x4 through dust-choked villages. Lakwena was situated amid an array of huts and tents clustered together and surrounded by a large circular fence of wooden stakes. She lived there much as I imagined she had in Uganda, surrounded by an adoring legion of men at her beck and call.

Somehow she didn't seem surprised to see me. A pair of tall, lean young men in flowing robes led me into the largest of the compound's huts, where Lakwena sat on a throne-like platform. Maps and artwork covered the walls. In a rambling, often incoherent conversation that stretched through the afternoon, Alice Lakwena tried to explain to me the spiritual journey that had led her to the battlefield, and ultimately exile.

"I am going home when the time comes," she told me, confidently. "I already wrote to be allowed back home. There has been no response, though. When I was in Uganda, I received the spirit, and the spirit took me and I was alive. In 1985, December, the group came to me. The spirit asked them not to fight in Kampala. 'They must take their guns and go.' The spirit ordered them not to kill civilians," referring to the LRA. "You don't kill civilians; you don't kill prisoners of war. Everything that connects to the movement or Kony is not me," she observed. "Me, I was fighting the government, not civilians. These are the commandments given by God. This is what I was following in the bush.

"Evil was occurring because [Kony and his followers] were ordering the spirit to go faster," she continued. "I was not expecting to come here, to Kenya. I want to see the [Ugandan] government. No response. A lot of people in my area [of Acholiland] are dying of the AIDS disease. If I go home, I will cure them. Why will they not let me go back home to cure them?

"And what about Joseph Kony? They are keeping him well in a beautiful house. It is the UNHCR and the Kenyan government that can tell you about him. He is well kept in Sudan."

Following my visit with Alice Lakwena in Kenya, I felt prepared to witness the surreal horror that was everyday life in northern Uganda. Departing from Nairobi and traveling to the Ugandan capital of Kampala, I was determined to find some understanding of how the distortion of faith had allowed so much havoc to be inflicted on thousands of Ugandan children, turning them into killers who could take the lives of family members and friends.

ANOTHER COUNTRY: LIFE IN NORTHERN UGANDA

As the LRA waged a relatively low-level conflict through the mid- to late 1980s, Museveni set about rebuilding the country. The history of the Lord's Resistance Army is punctuated by innumerable abductions and civilian attacks of unimaginable savagery, which truly means something in a nation that endured Idi Amin. Children's abductions began in 1987. The Sacred Heart Girls Boarding School in the town of Gulu was the first target. The majority of the 580 advanced-level students attending the school were from the districts of Gulu and Kitgum. In June of that year, several girls were taken from their dormitory. A year later, eighty-eight more girls were whisked away by attackers in the night. The last one occurred in 1991, when forty-three students were abducted, with two killed in the process. A Sudanese girl who attended Sacred Heart was kidnapped on her way to school and reportedly became a leader in Kony's movement.

On April 17, 1995, a group of three hundred LRA soldiers entered the trading center and town of Atiak, in the Gulu district. Easily overpowering the local home guard, the insurgents marched most of the civilians out of the area. The following day under direct orders from Kony, LRA soldiers (dressed in uniforms later identified as being Sudanese) separated from the rest those men and women deemed elderly or sick. Turning to the remaining captives, primarily kids and pregnant women, the commanders said, "What good are they now? What use do they have to the movement?" Moments later, they murdered 155 people with machetes, pangas, and rifles. The next day, eighty more civilians were killed. It was the largest single massacre by the Lord's Resistance Army. Already at an impasse with the Sudanese government, which he blamed for supporting Joseph Kony, Ugandan president Museveni broke off diplomatic relations.

In the ensuing years the LRA continued its incursion into northern Uganda to raid towns for supplies and abduct children. At the same time, the Sudanese government pushed Kony to engage in more combat with the Sudanese People's Liberation Army (SPLA) and Dinka tribesmen who oppose the government in Arab-dominated, Khartoum-based southern Sudan. Abductions such as the one at Aboke continued as well.

Two years after the attack at Atiak, 250 LRA fighters came into northern Uganda to re-arm an LRA contingent that needed weapons. The cache was buried in Kitgum district. Some time earlier, residents in the area who knew of the guns' location notified the UPDF, which seized possession of the weapons. Incensed, Joseph Kony sent his ranks in as avenging angels. Over five days, 437 men, women, and children were killed. The rebels were given instructions to kill anyone over the age of fourteen and take as many young girls as possible. Leaflets were dropped with red lettering. They read: "We the LRA don't want the life of people in the rural areas. Go to Kitgum town or Rwakitura [Museveni's home village]. If you resist the cure is only death penalty."

"He's a madman," said one former captive whom I met after a few days in the north. "When I arrived in the Sudan and met him, he was ordering his soldiers to execute small children by firing squad." For several years, the youth had been an escort for Kony, following military training.

"Very seldom would he ever show kindness," she continued. "There were many times when we children would have no food. [Kony] would send a vehicle to bring back supplies for him and his commanders. So he was happy and would just walk around greeting people and so on. If you were a boy and suspected of having a friendship with a girl, they would kill you in an instant." Girls who were kidnapped wind up becoming "wives" to Kony and his staff. On occasion, he would go to a particular boy or girl and say that a spirit had labeled him or her a traitor or potential escapee, and then have another child murder the one "labeled" by the spirit.

The military camp where Kony was based was apparently very large, having a multitude of small huts. Approximately five thousand to ten thousand rebels were housed there. Kony's quarters, an iron-roof house, sat exactly in the middle. Nearby was a much larger grass hut for his wives, numbering between thirty and sixty women. Each night he called in a different one to satisfy his needs. It was unknown how many children he'd sired by these teenage girls, but some of them were soldiers in the LRA.

According to accounts related by children I met at trauma centers in Gulu and prior reports, Joseph Kony spent most of his days sitting by the radio listening for information from his officers. Several dozen adult commanders were believed to be serving with him. After eating breakfast, he walked around the camp checking on the status of the sick and wounded. Those who are unable to fight were sent to a military hospital in Juba run by the Sudanese government. No Sudanese lived in the LRA compound, but some did visit regularly and ask to learn the Acholi language. Three youths at the humanitarian World Vision International center in Gulu had been sent there after their capture and said that Kony sold many children to the Arabs in exchange for guns. "In the last three years or four years, we've been involved in the rehabilitation and reintegration of formerly abducted children in Uganda," explained Kofi Ahgen, who was the country director of World Vision International in Uganda when I first traveled to that nation. Created by an organization built on faith, World Vision's center had a reception and psychotherapy program based in Gulu. Children in the program spent a period of about three weeks learning to accept what had happened to them and understand that they had been abducted and forced to do what they did. After they were reasonably adjusted and there was relative calm in their home communities, the youths were reintegrated.

"We make sure that their communities have a good understanding of what they have gone through and how they feel, to receive them with open hands, instead of accusing them of the atrocities they have committed," continued Ahgen. "For those who are older and those who can't go back to school, we feel a sense of responsibility and take them to another World Vision center below the Nile where they can get some skill training. Of course, there is a third part of the rehabilitation process, which is the community outreach where volunteer community counselors have been trained to receive and care for the young people. You can't keep them at a center too long because it is too expensive and donors are becoming very rare. We put a lot of emphasis on the community involvement; there must be an adaptation to local customs and traditions with respect to this problem of former child soldiers. It is an interesting situation because the young people and their families are making a transition from traditional practices. In a healing situation we cannot ignore that. They are also very church-oriented people, either Roman Catholic or Anglicans, so it is very important that the parts of them which respond to religion and modernity must be addressed. When there is pressure on a newly arrived young person, it is mostly from the traditional side. Our experience is that there are certain elements in African practices and religion that negate people's sense of security, and we do not encourage that in our program."

At the time of my first visit to Uganda, World Vision had been operating for twelve years in the northern region of the country, assisting more than four thousand children returning from the war. Joining World Vision's efforts in Gulu and Kitgum were other international groups such as Red Barnet (Danish Save the Children) and the International Rescue Committee (IRC), which operated a program for reintegrating children back into civilian life that was among the most respected locally.

If I needed a visual image of the human destruction caused by Kony and his minions, visiting the Gulu Orthopedic Workshop one afternoon gave it to me. A tiny wooden building resting on a slight incline, the place was part convalescence center, part woodworking shop. As I walked up to the building, I heard a high-pitched whirring sound coming from within. It sounded like someone was cutting up pieces of wood. Peering through an opening, I could see several men shaping prosthetic legs and limbs, which were then laid to rest against the walls. Several of the workers had badly scarred faces, some without lips or ears.

On the front porch a boy on crutches hobbled away from the workshop. Other wounded men and boys sat out in front on chairs or leaned inside the workshop, waiting for limbs or just curious. I walked over to one thin teen sitting on a bench with his crutches next to him. He was missing one of his legs below mid-thigh, the casualty of a raid.

"Since I am handicapped, I cannot farm," he told me. "My future may not be so good. If I return to my village, the rebels and the government forces may see me as a risk."

Owo Peter was one of the most unforgettable young people I met during my time in Gulu. He'd been snatched by members of the Lord's Resistance Army several years before we met. "Tell us everything, or you will die," the rebels had said to him. At World Vision's Gulu center he recounted the story to me of his experience with the LRA. We sat on old wooden desks across from each other in an empty classroom. It was a scorchingly hot day, and the high-pitched buzz of children playing outside filled the dust-choked air. Like Peter, they were receiving trauma counseling and educational preparation for the uncertain world outside the center's gates.

The guerillas had taken him from his home in the village of Odek in northern Uganda. He'd been working with the arts and crafts he sold along the roadside. Somehow the raggedy group of teens knew Peter had once been in the local home guard. In the bush six of them were chosen to torture him with panga sticks. As the guerillas moved with him and other captives, several commanders singled him out again for a beating with tree limbs. Ten grunts were chosen to lash his back, torso, and legs. The prisoners were headed to southern Sudan, where the rebel camp awaited. Peter survived the journey despite his severe wounds, but seven others didn't make it. When they arrived, he was taken to the top rebel leader, who was told that Peter was "UPDF," or a member of the Ugandan government forces. Pausing for a moment, the mysterious figure replied, "It is now upon us whether we're going to kill you or you're going to survive."

Though suffering from constant hunger, Peter did live and stayed at the rebel outpost for the next four years. His captors sent him, with very little training, into major battles with the SPLA, another rebel group based in Sudan but supported by the Ugandan government. The rebel head never spoke to him again, but Peter often saw him just listening to the radio. After his ordeal was over, he was uncertain how many people he'd killed.

When he was shot in the arm during an incursion, he saw his opportunity to escape. After a period in the Lacor Hospital in Gulu, he was brought to the staff at World Vision. "I didn't think I would live," he told me in a strained voice. "I can't return to my village because they would attack the family. If I am caught now, they will kill me with no explanations." The man to whom Peter was brought his first day in captivity was Joseph Kony.

Each night before going to sleep, he said a prayer in which he intermingled Protestantism with Catholicism and Acholi spirituality. Perhaps in deference to his Sudanese masters, there were days in which he and other leaders knelt down as if bowing in the direction of Mecca. Having designated Friday rather than Sunday to be the Sabbath day, Kony gathered the children around his hut to teach them his proverbs. "Don't worry. We're going to overthrow the government," he would say. "You're going to help us with that. It's better that you not run away, because if you do, the government soldiers are going to kill you and your families. So don't fear; stay with me here. Don't try to run away. If you run away and we catch you, we're going to kill you."

Wherever Kony traveled, a white folding chair was brought along for him to sit on. In order to renew his spiritual powers, he reportedly made annual treks to the Ato Hills in Uganda. Many years ago the Acholi engaged in brutal warfare with the colonizing British. Decades later, people said the rivers there flowed with blood.

He would allegedly ascend to the highest of the hills and lie down under the hot sun for days. A blanket of red termites was allowed to cover him, slashing deeply into his skin, and the oil from a plant called Yao was spread over his body. Afterward he entered a cave on the hill and stayed in seclusion for weeks on end.

In the early years of Kony's movement, he claimed to be led by a "spirit staff" comprised of a Sudanese woman, who was his chief of operations; a Chinese deputy chief, who oversaw a nonexistent jeep contingent; the spirit of the leader of the West Nile Bank Front, another Ugandan rebel group; and an American named Jim Brickey, who served alongside soldiers of the LRA on the condition they obey Joseph Kony.

"People were saying he was possessed by a spirit when he was praying on top of a mountain," said the former escort. "During these occasions children were not allowed to follow him. I'm not sure if the hills in Uganda were the Ato, but I know he went there three times in the years I was with them."

The directives that Kony gave to children in combat were even more absurd than the spiritual proclamations in the camp. Often guided by dreams or spiritual signs, he sent them into battle unarmed. When moving toward an objective, commanders forced them to march in a single file and essentially act as shields. Anyone who dropped their weapons, took cover during a fight, or retreated was killed.

"When you go to fight, you make the sign of the cross first," said Stephen, a seventeen-year-old boy interviewed by Human Rights Watch in its 1997 report *The Scars of Death*. "If you fail to do this, you will be killed. You must also take oil and draw a cross on your chest, your forehead, and each shoulder, and you must make a cross in oil on your gun. Also, you take a small stone, you sew it on a cloth and wear it around your wrist like a watch. That is to prevent the bullet that might come, because in battle it is acting as a mountain. So those people on the other side will look at you, but they will see only a mountain and the bullets will hit the mountain and not hurt you.[1]

"You also have water, they call it clean water and pour it into a small bottle," he continued. "If you go to the front, you also have a small stick and you dip it into the bottle and fling the water out. This is a river that drowns the bullet that might come to you.[2]

For its part, the government often acted inconsistently and sometimes heavy-handedly in its approach to the struggle with the LRA. One horrible example occurred in 1995, when Joseph Kony sent a group of rebels into Kitgum from northern Uganda to abduct 180 boys. Encountering UPDF forces, the LRA group lost three hundred through escapes during clashes. The following day another one hundred got away. As the commander marched the remaining kids back to Sudan, a government helicopter spotted the retreating column from the air. Rebels shot at the Russian-made craft, which opened fire with its machine turrets. Of the fifty-six bodies recovered, thirty-eight were children whose hands were bound behind their backs.

A journalist who visited the site in the aftermath spoke with a UPDF commander watching the burial of the children's bodies in a mass grave. "I still don't care [that they were children]," said the officer, an Acholi. "If they had crossed over into the Sudan, they would have come back as rebels."

Most of the residents of Gulu whom I met held little more than contempt for the government forces, instead of seeing them as protective saviors. They questioned why the LRA has held the government at bay for over a decade. Corruption, lack of will, and meager pay were all considered factors. The average foot soldier in the UPDF brought home about $100 a month, with home guard members earning an embarrassing $9.

Many of the so-called wives of troops in the barracks were young girls from Gulu and surrounding villages.

Late one particularly hot afternoon, I spoke with Major Wyncliffe, an intelligence officer with the UPDF Fourth Army Division. He argued for the wide success the military has enjoyed in its counter-insurgency effort against the LRA and the restrained tactics that have prolonged the war. "There was one chance in 1997 to capture Kony during a raid on an LRA camp, but he managed to escape back to the Sudan." According to Wyncliffe, 862 civilians were killed by the LRA in the past two years, and four thousand children under the age of eighteen were abducted.

At the barracks a number of LRA youth sat on the grass outside Wyncliffe's offices. They had been recently captured and were waiting to be debriefed by military handlers. I spoke to one woman in a smaller splinter-group of prisoners under a tree. They were being watched over by a handful of UPDF soldiers wearing camouflage T-shirts and jackets.

She had been fighting with the LRA for five years, since she was thirteen years old. The rebels had taken her from her home while she was having dinner with her family. The biggest challenge she faced was hunger, but the commanders had more subtle weapons as well.

"We were told that when we came out, the government would kill us," she explained to me. "They created a lot of fear. Those who tried to escape were battered to death. I saw at least fourteen receive this fate. When I was abducted, I was a very young girl, so they gave me to a man who made me his wife. After that, I was a woman."

"The UPDF has a concept called 'minimum reasonable force,'" Major Wyncliffe explained. "This is to cause minimal havoc to the community, because if we came in with tanks, the war would be over. With the stage we're at now, this conflict is over; the gun war is over. The international community should come in."

The major went on to explain that the UPDF has been directed to subdue as many rebels as they can and rescue children. "[The LRA] can terrorize people and then run back and hide," he continued. "If we were allowed into the Sudan, this war would be over, but our constitution does not allow us. We don't consider these abducted children to be the enemy."

One person who might have strongly disagreed with that statement was James Otto, Secretary-General of the Gulu-based Human Rights Focus. A former political prisoner of the Milton Obote regime, Otto maintained a file cabinet with over six hundred annual complaints of human rights abuses by members of the UPDF. "The civilian population has always been a pawn in this war," explained Otto. "They've [the UPDF] become more of an occupational army, killing citizens with impunity. It gives the wrong signal that perhaps a plan is being taken to eliminate people."

Okumu Ronald Reagan (named by his parents for the American whom they most admired), a member of parliament in the Gulu district, felt the same way and pointed to a greater risk if military violations go unchecked. "Kony has always said that the LRA is being blamed for acts that they did not do," he noted. "The more abuses committed by the army, the more credibility he gains."

ST. MARY'S GIRLS

The single largest abduction of children by the LRA occurred in the fall of 1996 at St. Mary's College in Aboke. One hundred and thirty-nine girls were taken. I spoke with Sister Rachele Fassera in Gulu, just outside of a rehabilitation camp called GUSCO, supported by Red Barnet. Two years after the abduction, she was still devastated by what had happened that night, grasping her rosary beads and softly crying with her head lowered to the ground as she spoke. St. Mary's was a boarding school in a village area about twenty-five miles from the border of the Gulu district. The rebels can walk a straight path there from Gulu. The staff had requested protection from the army, and a dispatch of soldiers had stood near the school since 1991. Even then, the nuns sent the girls to sleep outside, to make an escape into the bush easier.

Following an attack on the school in the spring of 1989, Sister Rachele Fassera, a forty-three-year-old nun with the Comboni Missionaries from Crenola in northern Italy, set out to meet the rebels the next day. Before she could make it, the guerillas ran into some government soldiers. Six of the abducted girls managed to escape, and three more joined them several months later. The one who never returned was presumed to have died in a fight. After that incident, St. Mary's was always a target for the Lord's Resistance Army. Sister Rachele and her colleagues focused on the safety of their students from then on.

At the end of September 1996, the government soldiers were moved temporarily about fifteen miles away from the school. It didn't take long for the rebels to learn that St. Mary's was unguarded. The sisters at St. Mary's realized the girls were in danger when nineteen soldiers came back to protect them on October 8. The following day they had to return to their post, but Sister Rachele was promised they would be back that night. All day Fassera and the others waited for the soldiers' return, but they never came. The girls were sent to bed inside. At 2:15 the next morning, a nightwatchman came to Sister Fassera's window and told her the rebels were on the campus. Years later, she would describe what happened that night in Aboke as "a gift from the Lord," for making her strong enough to share the pain of the girls' families.

"My first thought was the girls," she told me. "I went to call the administrators. I didn't wake up the elderly sisters. I said, 'The rebels are here; let us go get the girls.'"

As she and another nun, Sister Alba, ventured through the dark night, the entry gate was still lit up, leading them to think the barrier had not been penetrated or broken through. As they walked toward the dormitories, however, they were surrounded by the rebels. After the 1989 incident, they had put steel doors on the dormitory doors and steel bars on the windows. If the two women faced the rebels, they would have been forced to open up the dorms so the attackers could pluck as many victims as they wanted. The nuns trusted their salvation to the bars and steel doors.

"We called the elder sisters, and we threw ourselves in the grass," continued Sister Fassera. "We had just reached the grass when we began hearing the banging by the rebels. We were there on the grass, praying, when one voice of the girls inside started screaming."

The intruders burnt the school's car, parked in the courtyard. At some point they left, but not until the first daylight did the nuns get up. A small, frightened group of students—the youngest in the school—came up to them.

"Are you all here?" Sister Fassera asked them.

With tear-filled eyes, one of them replied, "The rebels have taken all of us!" "You can't imagine what we felt when we heard that," she told me, as she thought all of the students had been abducted by the LRA. It turned out that many were not.

She and Sister Alba went to check on one of the senior students' dormitories. The rebels had mistaken it for a food store because there was maize under the verandah. The eighty girls inside remained quiet and safe throughout the siege. Through the windows they saw many of their classmates being led away into the night by guerillas. The rebels broke through the walls, removed the steel-barred windows, and used them as ladders to enter and force the girls out.

They'd also tried to bend the steel bars, but they couldn't, so the guns and bombs they carried were flashed to scare the students into cooperating.

One senior student opened the door of her dormitory, while those in the two other senior dorms refused the fighters entry. In response, they broke through the windows and snatched the students inside.

"When I saw the wall, I said to Alba, 'I will follow them and look for the girls,'" recounted Sister Rachele. "I went to change clothes and put seven hundred Schilling from the office in my bag because I thought, 'If I give them money, they will give me the girls.' Then, I asked Alba and the teachers to accompany me on the road. At that point, there were two [male] teachers coming, so I asked one of them, Bosco, to come with me and follow the girls. Immediately he told me, 'Sister, let us go die for our girls.'"

Neither Sister Fassera nor Bosco knew the road, but the day before had been Uganda's Independence Day. The school had given biscuits, sweets, and soft drinks to the girls. The rebels had taken the treats and ate them as they traveled, so Rachele and Bosco had only to follow their crumbs to find them.

They set out at seven o'clock in the morning; it took them three and a half hours to reach the girls and their captors. As they climbed a hill, they could see them on an opposing hill. Rachele waved to them, and one of the guerillas ordered them to raise their hands, as thirty hardcore fighers of the Lord's Resistance Army came over with weapons aimed.

They wanted to know who the two pursuers were. "I am Sister Rachele Fassera," she said. Then it was her turn to ask a question. "Who is your commander?" One of the rebels stepped forward. "The first question he asked [me] was whether I knew Acholi," explained Sister Rachele. "I know a bit, so we started conversing. I brought out the money and said, 'Please give me the girls.'"

The commander asked one of his young soldiers to check her backpack. Digging around inside, he returned it to her and replied, "We don't want the money. I'll give you the girls. You come with us."

Filled with as much disbelief as hope, Sister Rachele and Bosco followed the commander, trailed by his fighters.

"I was holding my rosary, and he asked what are you doing," she recounted. "I said I am praying that you give me my girls. 'Don't,' he said. 'I will give you the girls.' Pulling a rosary out of his own pocket, he smiled and said, 'With this we are going to win.'"

The girls were sitting down on the path in groups of two and three in a long line with the rebels guarding them. She could see how sad the girls looked. She tried to smile at them but was met by tight expressions. They thought she was a prisoner, too. The commander, Mariano, told her to talk to the girls, and the group got up and continued walking together for two more hours. Finally, they came to an unused rail station, which she took to be a rebel resting spot or hideout.

Mariano told his soldiers to separate the St. Mary's students from the larger group of abducted girls who'd been taken from other schools and villages. Then he gave orders to one of the men to put out solar panels to charge the batteries of the radio. "I'm going to contact my superiors," he told Sister Rachele. She sat down with her students in a circle and waited for the commander to make a decision. While they were waiting, a government helicopter flew above them, and the group scattered. After it had gone, Mariano ordered everyone to their feet to continue walking.

"Leave me here with the girls," the tired nun asked Mariano. "No, you come," he replied. A local defense unit began firing at the guerillas, and again Mariano gave orders for everyone to spread out. Fassera, Bosco, the girls, and a number of armed rebels hid in a swamp until the shooting ended. Mariano engaged the opposing soldiers with thirty of his men in a firefight.

After a while the group in the swamp moved ahead and continued walking for four hours straight. The government helicopter returned, and the ritual was repeated over and over, with the girls and soldiers hiding, then moving, then hiding. Always, the girls and Sister Rachele were guarded by abducted children who'd been turned into soldiers, holding guns. If they felt the St. Mary's girls weren't hiding well enough, they'd appear with sticks to swipe at them.

By the time the drained group along with Mariano and his soldiers finally stopped, Sister Rachele assumed they were inside the Gulu district. Again Mariano separated the St. Mary's girls from the other abductees. Then he called forward two girls from the village and ordered the soldiers to beat them. Removing his dirty boots, he motioned for a young lady to bring him house slippers and a mat on which he and Sister Rachele sat. He sat on a chair, while the nun fit in next to his senior fighters.

"I was pleading, 'Please give me the girls,'" she told me, the rosary beads intertwined in her fingers as she fought back tears. "'Don't worry, Sister. I will give you the girls,' he said to me. For all this time, I was sure he would give me back the children. At a certain point, he said, 'You go wash, Sister.' A lady came up with a soap prepared with bananas. There was a banana plantation nearby. I thanked him and went to wash my hands and feet. While I was washing, he was choosing which girls he was going to keep."

Returning from washing, she thanked Mariano and asked for the girls so they could make the journey back to school. "What do you mean?" he answered her, feigning ignorance.

"Sister, he is not going to give us all the girls," Bosco told her.

"The girls are 139," said Mariano. Until that point, Sister Rachele hadn't known exactly how many of the abducted were hers. "I'll give you 109, and I keep thirty."

"Let *all* of the girls go," repeated Sister Fassera, straining her voice. "Mariano, give all the girls back and keep me."

"No," was the terse response from the commander. "But if Kony says yes, tomorrow they are all free. You can write him."

Pulling a piece of paper from her bag, she quickly scribbled, "Please release all the girls," and handed it to Mariano.

Mariano read the message, put the piece of paper in his pocket, and asked whether she had a picture of the Blessed Mother. She didn't, but she had a crucifix, which he took and put in his jacket. Kneeling down before him in desperation, Sister Rachele put her hand on his heart and begged one more time for the release of all the girls.

"No," he shot back. "Go and write down the names of those who are going to stay."

Shocked at the betrayal of his promise, as well as the task given to her, she slowly moved to the spot where the girls from St. Mary's huddled together. Then one by one all of them started pleading with her to save them.

"Sister, do not leave us here!"

"Sister, are you coming back tonight?"

"Sister, my mother is very sad."

"Sister, I have asthma."

She was able to write down only three names. One of the girls approached her and took the pencil and paper away. It was a senior student named Angela. "I will write our names," she said.

The distraught nun went back to the children, and Angela soon handed her the paper. Sister Rachele searched their uncertain faces, matching them with the names on the paper. She had them go collect their sweaters in order to move out with the group she would be allowed to rescue. When they returned a few moments later, one of the students who was on the list, Janet, had gone to hide with the girls who were being returned. Sister Rachele knew that if she had left only twenty-nine girls behind rather than the agreed thirty, Mariano would likely kill everyone in retribution. She had Angela bring Janet back over to the group that was staying.

"Please do not do this," she told the incredulous teen. "You put your friends in danger. 'I will not do it again,' she said."

After all the girls and Sister Rachele embraced each other, they knelt down and prayed together one last time. She told the girls who stayed not to look at them while they were leaving. It was the last time she would see most of them alive.

Sister Rachele returned to Mariano and asked him for a flashlight for the walk back through the night. It was another four hours before the group actually started heading back, sometime around midnight. Mariano told a ten-year-old village girl who'd been abducted to escort them back.

"As we came back, we got lost," Sister Rachele said to me, fingering her rosary while fat teardrops fell from her downturned eyes. "I came to know this afterwards, but as we left, it seems Mariano sent people to collect us back. After a while I saw a house, a big house, and I put all the girls inside the house while the teacher went to ask for help. He came back with two men, and we managed to reach the house of a local counselor in the Lango district. We kept the girls in the houses of these men for five hours, until early morning, reaching the school around midday. I think a message was sent to the headmistress and the parents that we were coming. They started running toward us when they saw the arrival. Can you imagine the scene when we returned, with those parents who found their daughter and those who didn't? From that moment on, we started the struggle to rescue the others, and it still continues."

Janet is still believed to be with the LRA in the Sudan. Angela is thought to have been lost fighting for the LRA in southern Sudan.

Two years after the incident, I met one of the other girls left behind, Josephine, then nineteen.

"When we saw one of our teachers and Sister Rachele, we at least had a hope of coming back to the school," she explained to me while we sat on the lawn of St. Mary's between classes. "Those who took us were very dirty—they looked like bushmen. As we were walking with them, if you tried to walk outside the line, they would push you roughly. They beat some girls and made us carry their loads for them, loads of things they had stolen, so we would not be able to run away from the line. If you tried to escape, they put you at gunpoint and beat you with the butt of their guns. I had thought I would be selected to come back like the others, but I was selected with the other twenty-nine girls that were not allowed to go with her that evening. Of course, I was not happy, but then there was nothing I could do. They threatened to kill us in front of Sister Rachele. Later, I was hurt doing some fighting, shot in the neck. The UPDF found me and brought me back."

FAR ON FAITH

Soon after the St. Mary's incident, the families of missing girls from the school formed the Concerned Parents Association to advocate for the girls' release and to raise global awareness about the issue of child soldiers. In the ensuing years, the organization would grow to include parents from different ethnic groups all over Uganda whose children had been taken.

Angelina Acheng Atyam, mother of one of the abducted girls at St. Mary's College and a founder of the Concerned Parents Association along with Ben Pere, became the international face for families dealing with this issue. She and I first met the same afternoon I spent with Sister Rachele at GUSCO, the Red Barnet–supported center.

A nurse and midwife, Angelina had six children—one boy and five girls, including Charlotte, who was the fourth born. At the time we met, her eldest daughter was twenty-three years old, and Charlotte was seventeen.

Around six o'clock in the morning the day after the abduction, a neighbor came to Angelina's window and told her the LRA had taken all the girls from St. Mary's College. She jumped out of bed screaming, not knowing what to do. Her husband lay in bed stunned. The neighbor came inside, and the two women sat and prayed. Angelina then decided she had to somehow get to the school as soon as possible.

When she arrived, she saw that all the windows had been broken, as Sister Rachele had found them the night before. The students' property, including slippers, clothing, and biscuits, were strewn about. Angelina thought the grass seemed trampled as if elephants had been there. She and the other parents heard that Sister Rachele was returning with the girls on the following day. Scanning the group and not seeing her daughter, she started screaming along with dozens of other distraught parents. There was no joy when Rachele returned, not even for the parents whose daughters were saved that day. Rain had created a single, discernible path out of the compound along which the rebels had led the girls in a single line. Angelina felt the ground was barren from then on. "It used to be that everybody in the north was a rebel, but then people stopped because they decided it wasn't worth it," Angelina told me. "Too many people got killed. Then the rebels started a new kind of rebellion. Can't the LRA see that their aggression against children, what they are doing is actuallly a misplaced aggression? I would say to them, 'Men, you killed, you raped, you pulled them away from us and remember: whatever reasons you have for your war, we put our case, our obligation before God.'"

When I visited Angelina in the summer of 1999, we spent an afternoon at her home just outside the main town in Lira. The setting was very lush, with lots of trees and grass. Several huts stood in the middle of a clearing, adjoined by a very large rectangular garden that had become overgrown. Angelina and I walked around the land, talking about ferns and other plants she enjoyed growing. She planted a number of the plants following

Charlotte's abduction. She also told me of a local tradition that any visitor who comes to the village for the first time is given a chicken. Warily, I took a loudly clucking and flapping one and put it in the back of my taxi, to the driver's amusement.

Finally, Angelina and I sat down to talk about Charlotte, the LRA, and the strength it took to maintain hope. Since Charlotte's abduction, Angelina had actually been able to arrange clandestine meetings with the LRA and herself or other members of Concerned Parents. At one point, the rebels even offered to release Charlotte, in the hope she would bring less publicity to what was happening in the country. She declined.

Her family couldn't enjoy the normal celebrations with Charlotte gone. Every time they heard the news of a missing child, it was like a jab to their hearts. The Christmas after her abduction was particularly hard. Charlotte couldn't get any messages out to them. The LRA, though, was well aware of Angelina's and the other parents' messages to the children and the world. They concealed the information from the children that their families were looking for them.

Angelina, who had delivered hundreds of babies as a midwife, was unable to deliver her own from captivity.

"Today, I had a girl who returned last December send a message," she said. "The message is very sad. Charlotte bore a baby boy last year. She had a difficult delivery and had to be taken to Juba—I don't know whether to a local doctor or a traditional doctor. Then she went back to the camp, where of course there was no medical help."

Pausing, Angelina smiled tightly and closed her eyes. Years of worry and stress revealed themselves through her taut face. "Charlotte was telling this girl, 'It was mommy who told me to go to school there,'" she continued. "Now she is away from the school, with the rebels, and I don't know what she is thinking. I hope and I don't want ever to lose that hope, to see her, wanting to support her."

The following year would have been her last year of school, Angelina explained. "My eldest daughter was sitting for her first degree course and made it. The other two sisters did not do very well. One of them missed getting government sponsorship to go to university, and another one had to take a lesser course to get sponsorship. I couldn't afford to pay for all the education. I had so much hope with Charlotte, but then she was taken away. So what we had planned for our children is no longer. The gap is there in the family, and things have never been the same. I wish the future generation of this country can do things differently from ours. We strongly believe as concerned parents that the barrels of the guns will not solve our problems.

"I was with other parents from Gulu district and the manager of the Ugandan electricity board when Charlotte was abducted," she recalled. "He tried to comfort me, but he himself was also weeping. I lost my senses; I was screaming. Sister Rachele looked tired and weak by the way she walked. I don't know how she picked up the strength. A woman saw us crying with another parent. She pulled my dress and said, 'Angelina, you have no faith. You did not pray enough. That's why your daughter doesn't come back.' That was a real provocation, but I think a good one. I made up my mind from that day no longer to cry, but raise up and do something. By traveling around I realized that many more parents are in a much worse situation than me. I made up my mind, and I will speak out for the voiceless. I will speak out until a solution to this problem is found. It's a very difficult situation. As Sister Rachele says, I wish we had talked about the LRA abductions much earlier. Fewer children would have been taken, and something could have been done much earlier, but we didn't till we were touched."

UNCERTAIN FUTURES

The things we do "two by two," wrote Rudyard Kipling, "we pay for one by one." In the case of Joseph Kony judgment may never come, at least not in this world. Nearly twenty years after the start of the conflict, though, an end finally seemed possible by 2004. Some observers felt that as long as Uganda backed the SPLA and Sudan backed the LRA, there wouldn't be an end. Despite a willingness to negotiate directly with other insurgencies, President Yoweri Museveni took no such public step toward the LRA, at least not until a former Acholi government minister and World Bank official named Betty Bigombe became actively involved in the fall of 2004.

"A North which is not peaceful is a threat to Uganda's future," explained Okumu Reagan. "A North which is underdeveloped because of the war is a threat to Uganda's future. The government blames our people for supporting the rebels, but if our people really supported the rebels they would not be committing atrocities against us.

"The challenge of northern Uganda has to be addressed," he continued. "Our people have been ambivalent; you have to survive."

I became friends with Betty Bigombe during phone conversations and visits to her office in Washington, D.C., in the course of researching this book. She arranged one of the only face-to-face meetings with Kony and top LRA commanders in the village of Awach. Despite great progress toward disarmament of the LRA, negotiations broke down because of what some people felt was sabotage and jealousy of Bigombe by the Ugandan army.

Museveni's attitude seemed to change from 1996, when he told a press conference, "Our work is to kill these people, and we shall crush them. I give [Kony] about seven months, and he will either be killed, his group wiped out, or captured." A meeting in Tehran, Iran, in November 1996 with Malawi, Sudan, and Uganda yielded little in the way of progress toward peace. Rumors of secret concessions and overtures were constantly subverted by Museveni's public statements.

A widely read study on the conflict in northern Uganda commissioned by the U.S. Agency for International Development (USAID) in September

1997 and popularly known as the Gersony Report, for its author, consultant Robert Gersony, recommended, among other things, the vigorous resumption of negotiations with the rebels, a human rights investigation of abuses by both sides, and a greater role in the process by the international community. John Nagenda, Museveni's media adviser at the time, responded to the report by telling reporters he was throwing it away.

One of the best chances for tempting Kony and his minions to leave the bush and put down their weapons was the Amnesty Act of 1998, which was supported in nearly every district of Uganda. It proposed legislation that would grant a general amnesty to all groups warring against the government, upon the condition arms were turned over to the designated authorities. The amnesty would not have applied to crimes such as rape, kidnap, or acts of genocide, for which Joseph Kony could certainly be prosecuted.

Many of the people I met in Gulu and Kitgum said that the only way of convincing him to surrender was guaranteeing his safety and immunity from prison. "An army is an entity," noted Okumu Reagan. "You can't give amnesty to the lower troops and not Kony."

The Acholi community has a ritual process of reconciliation that would allow Joseph Kony and his commanders to return home. When combatants stop their fighting to make peace, it was called *lacwec tye,* or "bending the spears."

"The safest way for them to come back would be to apologize, repent," said Charles Alai, an Acholi elder and former M.P. Sitting outside on the patio area of a downtown Kampala hotel, Alai explained why Joseph Kony would never face the wrath of his Acholi brethren, whom he's victimized for over a decade. "They must tell the people they are sorry and at the same time undergo the traditional reconciliation process, *mato oput.* If I know I've killed a relative of yours, I must say that I'm sorry and did it for this and this reason. Because I've come to confess, you may not kill me. A certain amount must also be paid in animals, usually goats, and now money."

The Acholi believe that the spirit of a murdered person would haunt the murderer until reconciliation took place. It could not rest and without *mato oput,* the parents and family would feel that their loved one had died for nothing. "All the people who have been killed up until now have not been reconciled," noted Alai. "The traditional rites have not been performed."

Another element of *mato oput* involves drinking. There is a locally brewed beer, of which the perpetrator and the victim's family partake to signify a rapprochement. "There is a tree that grows in Acholiland which has a bitter juice," continued Alai. "To show that you are forgiven, you are made to drink this juice. Even if you are responsible for the deaths of many people, you still have to do this. If the person was a soldier, you still have to do it. Even if there are many, you have to do it, but the amount is not so much. It is a symbol."

There was some question as to whether any of Joseph Kony's siblings were alive. His father lived in anonymity just outside Kampala, and his mother was somewhere in western Uganda, possibly near the copper mining town of Kasese. A relative of the family told me that Kony murdered a sister of his not long after he began his movement because she was romantically involved with a soldier in Museveni's army.

Shortly before my first trip to Uganda, Joseph Kony wrote a letter to Okumu Ronald Reagan, remarkable for its conciliatory tone. It wasn't the first time he'd used the parliamentarian to send a message to Acholi leaders and the greater society. Several of his top commanders had written as well, and all the messages had Arabic script emblazoned at the top. Okumu Reagan showed it to me.

In his letter dated October 25, 1998, Kony wrote:

> I thank God for keeping all of you up to now. I also thank the Almighty for allowing me to write this. My brothers and sisters, I am not happy, because ignorance has destroyed our home. . . . Now, you people still with Museveni today, why don't you lead our people in the right path? This war is not an Acholi war. Kony is fighting for you to liberate you. I don't want my tribe to be used to be insulted.
>
> We have to fight [Museveni] until he's overthrown. I know we in the Lord's Resistance Army are going to throw out Museveni. Time for war is time for war. Death and many sufferings will definitely be there. . . . The end of Museveni's movement is close. . . . You have rejected Kony. You have not supported us, but we alone can overthrow Museveni. Let us unite and end this war in Acholi. I am ready to meet with you, anywhere, anytime, anyplace to bring an end to this conflict. God Bless You.

Not everyone believed Kony would get off so easily. "I [do] think people would openly forgive Kony for the sake of peace," replied one Ugandan journalist whom I asked. "But later, when he was back in society walking around, many people would want to hurt him. When this thing is over with, that will be the real beginning for the Acholis."

If Joseph Kony and senior officers do not face justice in a Ugandan court, they very well might outside the country. The International Criminal Court in Rome, which became active in July 2002, issued its first arrest warrants in 2004, naming Joseph Kony and a dozen other LRA officers for war crimes. Among the charges is the illegal use of children as soldiers.

HOMECOMINGS

On July 19, 2004, Charlotte Atyam awoke in her tent inside an LRA camp. She thought someone was talking to her in the middle of the night, around 2 AM. The voice told her, "Today, you go home." She wondered who it was, and early the next morning she knelt to pray.

"God, if it was your voice, talk to me," she said.

At eight o'clock the groups of child fighters were moving out to a different location, somewhere in remote northern Uganda. Usually Charlotte had five bodyguards, one in front, one on each side, and two behind. That morning, though, she walked a few yards and realized no one was guarding her. She moved to the left as she realized everyone else was moving to the right. Charlotte, who was fourteen when she was taken, was forced during her captivity to "marry" an LRA commander with whom she had two children. She fled with the elder of her children, a six-year-old boy named Reynolds. The other child had been lost during an air raid by the Ugandan army a month before.

Alone in the bush she met two other groups from the LRA. None of them bothered her or asked her any questions. She continued walking for six hours before coming across farmers cultivating their land.

They asked her, "Who are you, and where are you coming from?"

"I'm escaping from the rebels," she replied, matter-of-factly.

Immediately the people left their work and ran from her. They were scared and thought maybe the rebels were following her, which was true. Fortunately, they ran home and reported the encounter to the chief of security personnel in that area. The official in charge of security was also a member of the Concerned Parents Association. When he realized that Charlotte was Angelina's daughter, he managed to find a phone number to tell Angelina what was happening.

"We were having a meeting in the office of the Concerned Parents Association in Lira," recalled Angelina. "When I received the call, I thought it was too wonderful to be true. At the beginning, I didn't know what to say. He told me, 'The girl is here.' He even said that he was taking her to the barracks in Pader, because that is the routine when children return. So, I immediately left Lira for Pader."

The next morning Angelina was joined by nearly two dozen Concerned Parents Association members from the area in her walk to the barracks.

"They took their time bringing her to me," she noted. "But the moment I saw her, it was too wonderful. I started screaming, and everybody was wondering what was wrong. Her little son, Reynolds, was left behind as we celebrated. He had gone into a social worker's office. I know he wondered, 'Who is that woman that my mother abandons me for?' The social worker told the boy, 'Here is your grandmother.' In our vocabulary, though, 'grandmother' has no meaning. That was my child, too."

Unlike her trip to St. Mary's eight years before, which she saw as a "terrible time," the reunion with her fourth-born daughter held tremendous joy and excitement for Angelina. Charlotte's other son was ironically discovered the same day as Charlotte. He was held in a different military barracks but ultimately identified by social workers interviewing him and learning of Charlotte's escape. Though he had been named by the LRA, Angelina decided to call him Miracle.

Whatever happiness she found that day was bittersweet. At that point, six of the St. Mary's girls abducted by the LRA with Charlotte eight years before were still lost: three were in captivity, and three were dead. The rest had returned, but the thousands of others across northern Uganda had not. It was even more difficult for Angelina to do work with the Concerned Parents Association. She and her family could not give thanksgiving prayer and celebrate Charlotte's return. Angelina felt too much sympathy for the many members whose children were still missing.

"Charlotte didn't really change a lot, but she talks a little less than before," Angelina told me. I spoke to her on my mobile phone while she was in Lira, shortly after her first Christmas with Charlotte in many years.

"We can still talk as before, but there has been some change. There is discomfort because of these children born in captivity. For me I have to use all opportunities to get the children released. Sister Rachele did a wonderful thing, but for us it is not a question of some children being freed, but of all the children. We must make use of any opportunity we get to tell the world what we are going through. I will go another mile if necessary to make this happen.

"I spoke to Sister Rachele three days ago," she continued. "She is always happy when a child returns. Maybe it is good she has left Uganda. I know that since the day she left the thirty girls behind, she has never been the Rachele we knew before. I think she died many times. She died with the children she left in captivity and the children who die every day in the war. I don't know whether Sister Rachele will recover fully."

Twenty years after arriving in Uganda, Sister Rachele Fassera was called back to Rome by her superiors. I spoke to her in late 2004, for the first time in five years, amazed that she remembered me with apparent fondness. Since October 1996, a memorial ceremony is held annually to honor the girls who were taken, returned, or lost. The school administrators and the Concerned Parents Association also formed a tribute to Sister Rachele in creating a rehabilitation center for returned child soldiers in her name.

"Now that I am here, the superior has asked me to do service for this congregation in Rome," she explained. "It was not easy to leave Uganda, but maybe I am traditional. In obedience I find God's will, and this is what I cherish most. When the superior asked, I objected to this type of work, because I didn't know if I was capable. I will try. I would have never asked to leave Uganda or Africa. Aboke was my life. But when I was asked, I said, 'Yes, if this is what you are asking me, I will do it. Even with tears.'

"With the experience of Aboke, the happiness is the witness inside of us," she said to me. "With what happened, I truly became a Comboni

143

sister. One of the tenets of Comboni Missionaries is to make common cause with the people, to live with and participate fully in their joy and their sadness. This is what the Lord gave me in Aboke. This tragedy opened me to the suffering of all humanity, not only the people I know."

Incredibly, the fragile Italian woman I had met and whose courage inspired me years later found grace through her experience in Aboke and the struggle that followed. For her, it meant fulfillment as a missionary and as a human being.

NOTES

1. Rosa Ehrenreich, *The Scars of Death: Children Abducted by the Lord's Resistance Army in Uganda* (New York: Human Rights Watch, 1997), 23.

2. Ibid., 24.

5

In Search of Ghosts in Afghanistan: An End, of Sorts, to a Journey

IN THE WINTER OF 2004, I went to Afghanistan, of all places, looking for hope. Inasmuch as this book was a journey toward understanding the lives of child soldiers and war-affected children, it was also a personal one for me to try to understand why I was so fixed on following the lives of children and youth as a journalist and why I'd chosen to do a seemingly quixotic book. Ultimately, I never found the answer to those questions, and maybe I never will. That was a realization I didn't discover until several years into the project, which had to end at some point, despite my best efforts to prolong it—blowing deadlines, getting sick, or looking for distractions wherever I could find them.

After much internal debate, I decided to make a five- to six-week trip to Afghanistan only a few weeks before I actually left on the journey. Normally I didn't talk with my friends or family about my trips before taking them. And I certainly didn't express any fears or concerns, if I had them. My journey to Afghanistan was different.

Of all the countries I'd decided to focus on, Afghanistan held the greatest sense of dread for me, even before the 9/11 attacks. When I originally decided to do this worldwide investigation, Afghanistan was among the countries I had in mind, but at one point I dropped it from the list out of reluctance. I called the situation there a "boutique conflict," because by the time I arrived, it was no longer a high-level conflict and the overwhelming bulk of the international press corps had returned home or, more likely, moved on to Iraq. I'd never been to that part of the world before, but my instincts told me not to do it. I chose to write about the Palestinian Territories instead, but I dropped that, too, after a brief visit in the summer of 2001. For reasons of tone and politics, I made the decision to stick with Afghanistan. Then my daughter was born, and the 9/11 attacks occurred.

More often than people will admit, being a parent demands facing and compromising with fear, either for your children's well-being or for your own. In my case, I constantly felt afraid whenever I left home on reporting trips. Common sense would have told me to avoid going to conflict zones after becoming a parent, but I actually ended up going more than before. What changed was that I became overly conscious of the possibility of something happening to me, whereas before, I acted as if I didn't care.

Just past the age of thirty, after ruining a marriage and nearly losing my life from a cardiac emergency and my mind from post-traumatic stress midway through this project, being a father was one of the few things left at the end of this journey. It also gave me greater insight into what the families I'd met in Africa, Latin America, and Asia had gone through when their sons or daughters were lost to war. I overrode my instincts and went to Afghanistan, against the advice of friends and family.

THE MARTYR

Three months after the September 11 attacks in New York and Washington, D.C., by individuals linked to the Al-Qaeda terrorist network, a thirty-three-year-old non-commissioned officer (NCO) named Nathan Ross Chapman became the first uniformed American soldier to die in combat in what was called Operation Enduring Freedom. Originally from a suburban community in Ohio, the barrel-chested soldier had served in the Persian Gulf War, Panama, and Haiti. His home unit at Fort Lewis, Washington, had not actually been sent into Afghanistan, but his skills as a communications specialist were much in demand. So he volunteered to go with a unit out of Fort Campbell, Kentucky.

He died in Khost, a sometime hotbed area of Islamic fundamentalism and anti-Western sympathy in eastern Afghanistan. A little more than two years later, another American "hero" lost his life there to friendly fire: Pat Tillman, the Arizona Cardinals football star who had quit professional sports to enlist in the military after the September 11 attacks. Khost, near the border of Pakistan and Afghanistan, is a no-man's-land when it comes to Western or American influence.

As tragic and unfortunate as Chapman's death was for his family—he left behind a wife and two children—I was as intrigued by his death as I was by who was suspected of killing him: a fourteen-year-old Afghan boy. With only a map and a vague idea of how to get there, I set my mind to finding Nathan Ross Chapman's killer.

Chapman had been a member of the lauded First Special Forces Group (Airborne), based out of Fort Lewis, Washington. Originally activated as a joint Canadian-American unit in July 1942, the unit was specifically created to carry out the riskiest of missions behind enemy lines. Participating in a number of campaigns during World War II in North Africa, France, and Italy (both at Anzio and in Rome), it was disbanded and reorganized several times in the succeeding decades, seeing particularly heavy action in Vietnam.

Chapman had been in-country since November 2001. Publicly reported accounts of what exactly happened to Chapman varied. One theory held that Chapman had been killed as a result of rivalries between two warlords in the heavily Pashtun region, Padsha Khan Zadran and Zakim Khan Zadran, unrelated but both members of the Ghilzai clan. A visit to Khost by an American delegation under the escort of Zakim Khan was seen as the United States favoring him over Padsha Khan. In retaliation operatives were placed to fire on the delegation, which arrived on January 3, 2002, by helicopter to survey physical damage from American bombing strikes and to gather intelligence from local leaders in the city of Khost on Osama Bin Laden and Jalaluddin Haqqani, a Taliban commander who was also wanted.

The day after their arrival, the delegation met with the two rival warlords and drove by truck to see the targets of two air strikes. Three vehicles filled with Zakim Khan Zadran's troops escorted them. After visiting a mosque that had been inadvertently hit months before on the first day of Ramadan, the convoy drove to the site of tank shelling by the Taliban, entering a sector controlled by Padsha Khan Zadran, the Mattah Chinah area of Khost. Dismissing warnings, Sergeant Chapman stood up in the bed of his pickup truck with a camera around his neck. Shortly after the group encountered hostile members of Padsha Khan's army, a volley of shots rang out, hitting Chapman in the legs and wounding a CIA agent sitting inside the truck.

Padsha Khan argued that the shots that killed Chapman came from behind a mosque fifty yards away and weren't fired by any of his men. Zakim Khan countered that the rounds were fired from directly in front of the convoy, where Padsha Khan's troops were located. In support of his assertion, Padsha Khan produced a fourteen-year-old boy who he claimed admitted to having fired the shots. The youth escaped from detention and fled into Afghanistan, according to news reports, but in response Padsha Khan grabbed up three of the youth's cousins to force them to bring him back. Later, it was said the three detainees were handed over to the American forces and taken to a military prison in Kandahar for interrogation.

Sergeant Chapman was the second son of Wilbur and Lynn Chapman, born at Andrews Air Force Base, Maryland, on April 23, 1970. His father was a veteran officer who'd been stationed at various bases across the United States and remained in the service for the first eight years of Nathan's life. When Wilbur left the military to work in business, he was transferred four or five times before Nathan graduated from high school. In the Chapman family the military influence was not particularly strong.

According to his brother Keith, two years older, Nathan was a thrill-seeker and slightly unfocused growing up. In 1988, his final year in high school near Dayton, Ohio, he surprised his family and friends by enlisting in the Army and quickly making the cut to become an elite member of the Rangers. Within a year he was deployed in the invasion of Panama.

I spoke with Keith at his home in suburban Maryland in the summer of 2004. "As a youth in school, he wasn't a motivated student," he told me. While Nathan had gone the military route, Keith pursued academic goals at Carnegie Mellon University. "He did present the military to my parents as a decision he had made, but I don't think they believed him when he announced it. I don't know where he got the idea or if my parents know from where he got the idea. The general consensus is that having done it was a good thing for him because of the discipline he lacked as a child. The difference between the services is not well-known to me, but it seems to me that if he had joined because of what my father had done, he would have joined the Air Force. I don't know that he had any particular goals."

In the ensuing years, Nathan married a woman named Renae and had two children, Amanda and Brandon. He also saw consistent action overseas in the Persian Gulf War, Haiti, and the Balkans.

That is all I knew about the life and death of First Sergeant Nathan Ross Chapman.

AN OLD THREAT FOR A NEW CENTURY

It has been estimated that at least 10 percent of the world's fighting forces are under the age of eighteen. Since the time of the Roman and Spartan Empires, children have been molded into combat-ready soldiers, all the way up to the Civil War and later, World War II, which saw the emergence of a formal cadre of trained children, the Hitler Youth. In Vietnam youths were used on suicide missions to ambush unsuspecting American GIs. But today, with the proliferation of light weapons and the range of low- to high-level conflicts emerging around the world, the percentage of kids in combat has been growing higher and higher.

Sadly, the United States has not always been the most constructive partner in achieving meaningful international action on the issue of child soldiers. The Machel Report, a 1996 study presented to the United Nations General Assembly, documented the suffering of millions of children because of war. It is my belief that U.S. intransigence on discussions of the Convention on the Rights of the Child, the International Criminal Court, and small arms control has hurt children caught up in armed conflict.

The CRC outlines in detail the rights of protection for children living in difficult circumstances, including conflict, disease, and displacement, as well as domestic rights related to their parents and caregivers. As mentioned in chapter 2, the United States is one of only two countries that have not ratified it. In 1995, President Bill Clinton signed the treaty, but the U.S. Congress has been unable to ratify it. Generally, the Pentagon and, on occasion, the State Department believe that the United Nations should not interfere in domestic American matters, such as how and whom the country recruits into the armed forces. Further, members of Congress have long doubted the wisdom of conferring special rights on children; this is particularly true of many conservatives, who view the convention as an assault on the "traditional family."

In January 2000, after six years of negotiation, progress was made with the passage of the Optional Protocol to the CRC. At the insistence of American and British officials, the 1989 CRC had set fifteen as the minimum age for recruiting soldiers. The Optional Protocol addresses the behavior of non-governmental and governmental armed groups but also applies a more stringent standard to non-governmental groups than to governments.

Three years ago delegates representing 160 countries voted in Rome to establish a permanent International Criminal Court (ICC) to try persons charged with committing war crimes, crimes against humanity, and genocide. As of November 2004, 139 nations had signed the ICC treaty, and forty-seven had ratified it, with only thirteen more ratifications needed to bring the court into existence.

The creation of the ICC is important for children because the court will provide a powerful deterrent to using children under the age of fifteen in war. The treaty also deems intentional attacks on schools a crime, provides special arrangements for children as victims and witnesses, and exempts children below the age of eighteen from judicial prosecution. The United States has been the most formidable obstacle to the ICC because of fear that U.S. officials or military personnel would be open to prosecution. The United States wants the accused's government to have veto power, which would essentially void the core aim of the ICC.

Small arms kill half a million people each year, primarily women and children. A recent target of America's military wrath, Afghanistan, is itself home to at least ten million light weapons, and in Africa illegal guns fuel the twenty conflicts now taking place. The United Nations has proposed a nonbinding accord to cut down on the numbers of submachine guns, assault rifles, hand grenades, grenade launchers, and portable missile launchers.

Most governments agree that steps should be taken to tighten up export regulations, to bolster the exchange of information on arms transfers, and so on, but the White House and a significant number of congressional members will not accept limits on the transfer of small arms to nongovernmental forces or controls on the domestic sale and manufacture of small arms. That resistance can be traced to concerns over the American ability to arm guerilla groups or military partners overseas, as well as the inevitable uproar of advocacy groups.

Following UN Resolution 1460 in January 2003, which called for all nations and groups using child soldiers to cease doing so, the London-based Coalition to Stop the Use of Child Soldiers compiled a report on countries still using child soldiers in the eight months after its passage. Out of seventeen countries targeted in the report (slightly more than half of the known locations where child soldiers exist), more than fourteen received or were slated to receive military aid from the United States, including Afghanistan, Colombia, Sri Lanka, Uganda, and Rwanda.[1]

Curbing the flow of small arms and weapons to nations where children are at risk of being recruited was a major recommendation of the Center for Emerging Threats and Opportunities (CETO), a Virginia-based institute sponsored by the Marine Corps Warfighting Laboratory in existence since 2002, and the only armed service studying the threat of child soldiers to U.S. armed forces. No special training or education on child soldiers is provided to enlisted personnel or commissioned officers by the Department of Defense.

In November 2002, CETO held a one-day seminar organized by retired army colonel Charles Borchini titled "Child Soldiers: Implications for U.S. Forces." Among the handful of lecturers was Major Jim Gray, a British Royal Marine who knew firsthand what it is like for a professional army to encounter child soldiers in the field.

"For the most part, Westerners cannot comprehend what it is like in many of the countries where children are fighting as soldiers," he noted. In 2000, a British military patrol on deployment in Sierra Leone was taken hostage by a militia composed essentially of children, because the commander would not open fire on them. A rescue mission two weeks later resulted in an estimated 150 deaths, including many youths. Major Gray served on a UN observer mission to Sierra Leone in 1999. "What is normal in these countries is far from anything that is normal in the West. In these countries, governments have broken down and are unable to enforce law and order, provide basic services such as water and electricity, or operate schools. Armed gangs, militias, and armies roam the cities and control traffic throughout the countryside. The citizens, especially the children, are victims to the disorder.

"Upon returning home, U.S. and Western forces may not be able to cope with normal life and may go through a period of post-traumatic stress disorder," he continued. (I myself suffered a mild form of this just in the process of researching this book.) "Many will be deeply affected by what they saw. U.S. and Western military leaders must prepare the forces for the kind of environment they will face before they deploy on operations. They also must go through the process of discussing and understanding what they were exposed to upon redeployment. Similar efforts will be needed with the family members of returning service members before they return."

In a report produced as a result of the seminar, CETO argued for, among other things, implementation of the Optional Protocol to the Convention on the Rights of the Child, support for the International Criminal Court, the protection of demobilized child soldiers, and the sensitization of American forces to the personal and moral consequences of confronting children on the battlefield, before and after deployment.[2]

THE HEART OF THE GAME

In late February 2002, after several stops and starts, I left for Afghanistan, sick with the flu and more than a little uncertain of finding any success. My spirits were dampened further when my flight to Kabul via Moscow was cancelled en route, stranding me for a day and a half. The Afghan airline was apologetic but not entirely helpful, putting me on a connecting flight from Moscow to Baku, Azerbaijan, where I sat for twenty hours in a sparse waiting area reading and rereading magazines I'd carried with me and talking to a contractor from Boise, Idaho, named Bill. He'd been working in Afghanistan for seven months by that time, but his cheeriness about the place failed to sway my skepticism.

The next morning we flew into Kabul and then made a mad rush to the conveyor belt carrying our luggage. Initially I was surprised at how international the place seemed. Americans, Europeans, Africans, and Latin Americans were all present in the airport. Many of them I assumed were contractors or employed by one of the hundreds of NGOs present at that time.

One of the first people I met after stabling myself in a guesthouse was David, an American graduate student working at the Afghan Human Rights Commission. In the month and a half I was in Afghanistan, he was my closest friend and saved me from going insane. One evening he explained the draw of Afghanistan, after I commented on the unusual number of foreign workers and soldiers present.

"There's a saying that missionaries, mercenaries, misfits, and the brokenhearted come to Afghanistan," he said, laughing. "If you don't know which one you are by the time you get here, you will when you leave. The Afghanis still haven't gotten over getting their asses kicked by Genghis Khan."

From the moment I arrived, I rarely saw the face of an Afghan woman, as most continued to wear the notorious burkhas or veils covering their hair and the sides of their faces. Women could go to school but couldn't walk down the streets with a man who was not a family member or spouse. They could not shake hands with a man or look into his eyes.

But I was also surprised by the hidden but well-known phenomenon of man-boy sexuality. Many of the boys who fought with the Northern Alliance during the war were thought to have been regularly used as sexual partners by the adult commanders. It is primarily a Pashtun tradition but does occur across ethnic lines.

Dry, landlocked, and extremely mountainous with no obvious natural resources of interest to the outside world, Afghanistan has been involved or surrounded by conflict for much of its history. Its value has always been in serving as a central trade route between the Middle East and Central and South Asia, most recently for opium and human trafficking. The British and Russian Empires fought for control over it in the so-called Great Game of the nineteenth century, and more than a hundred years later an invasion by the Soviet Union in 1979 plunged it into a perpetual civil war up through the September 11 attacks.

Following the withdrawal of the Soviet army and their support of a puppet communist regime in 1989, a U.S.-backed Islamic insurgency took control and eventually evolved into the anti-Western, terrorist-friendly Taliban government. The Northern Alliance was the Afghan opposition created in response to the Taliban and led by Masood, a charismatic figure who was assassinated on September 9, 2001, by suspected Taliban agents.

Had he lived, Masood arguably would have become president of Afghanistan. Instead, another Pashtun politician from Kandahar named Hamid Karzai was elected in October 2004.

Since the fall of the Taliban, Afghanistan has resumed its production of opium, which stopped after their ascendance to power. Today the nation is the world's largest supplier of the drug.

More than five million people have been displaced in the recent era of fighting since 1979, half of them children, and nearly two million Afghanis have died. Significantly, both the Northern Alliance and the Taliban used children, for the most part boys, throughout their struggles. Most of the adult men who fought the Taliban grew up fighting the Soviets as teenagers. According to the Coalition to Stop the Use of Child Soldiers, the Northern Alliance was recruiting children as young as eleven up to the time the United States became actively involved in the war. And in one incident an estimated one hundred Taliban child soldiers died in a battle with Northern Alliance troops at Mazar-i-Sharif.

Despite the prevalence of children in combat through the last spates of conflict in Afghanistan, the majority of its citizens think that only adults should be fighting. In the 1999 "People on War" study done by the International Committee of the Red Cross, 76 percent of people surveyed believed a soldier should be at least twenty years old, and even 67 percent of those fighting felt the same. Many religious teachers at *madrassas*, the fundamentalist Islamic schools from which many young recruits were drawn by the Taliban, also felt that no one below the age of twenty-five should serve, because that age was when people started "knowing about good and bad."[3]

Although accurate documentation on the numbers of children actively associated with armed groups is not available, UNICEF reported in mid-2003 that between five thousand and ten thousand young men, ages fourteen to eighteen, continued to fight in Afghanistan. They were attracted by promises of payment or education, by a desire to protect their own communities, or by the status and power of carrying weapons. Some joined voluntarily, but others were coerced under threat of death or injury. In some cases local commanders demanded that families provide a son to fill quotas imposed by regional commanders. Parents also sent their children to join armed groups for ideological reasons, and juveniles under eighteen joined up alongside their brothers or other family members.

During my time in Afghanistan, there were thought to be no imprisoned child soldiers, although a demobilization effort overseen by UNICEF was well under way. Minors were found at the detention center for Al-Qaeda and among Taliban suspects at the Guantanamo Bay camp in Cuba, and after clamoring by Human Rights Watch and other groups, a handful of youths had been released shortly before my trip to Afghanistan.

UNICEF was coordinating the disarmament and reintegration of thousands of child soldiers, both Taliban and Northern Alliance, throughout the country, but various NGOs were doing the hands-on process, including the International Rescue Committee, Radda Barnen, and the Christian Children's Fund.

"The Afghan concern for kids ends at around the age of five years old," one aid worker told me. "Young people are seen as a menace, in some way. In the field, these boys have more of a closed life. Many were recruited from *madrassas* in Pakistan. Now, the warlords are not turning over lists of kid soldiers. So there's no fully accurate way of knowing how many kids are present in a faction. There's also no broad analysis of social rights implications on different age groups, especially children. During the Taliban, there were no facilities for children to do things. The kids [boys] studied the religion and Taliban ideology more under the Taliban because there were no other diversions."

THE ROAD TO KHOST

Depending on who was running things in Kabul, the eastern province and village of Khost has undergone a series of popular names, including "Little Moscow" when the Soviet Union was influential, then "Little Kuwait" under the Taliban. When I visited, it was called "Small America." Khost is part of a group of tribal areas known as Greater Paktia, which includes Paktia and Paktia provinces.

In these areas, Arbeki, the village self-defense forces, which are obligatory for young men in the community to join, dictate the settling of disputes over land or personal crimes. The strength of areas such as Greater Paktia comes from the fact they're tribally governed by councils of elder leaders known as *shuras*. These tribal *shuras* are quite united and effective in policing their areas, even against rival groups. Young people who serve in the Arbeki are typically around fifteen or sixteen years old. These youths weren't being demobilized when I was in Afghanistan, but there was negotiation under way to begin that process. A lot of the adult male population in the tribal areas are migrant workers or live abroad, leaving the young men and boys to handle security. Because of the culture's gender dynamics, the idea of girls or women serving in uniform or carrying weapons was out of the question.

After weeks of overcoming my flu in Kabul and struggling to find a safe transport to Khost with an international aid group, I finally found someone willing to escort me and left early one cold morning in a white SUV with a driver and an Afghan relief worker. The organization was the only international agency working in Khost, a clear sign of the presumed risks awaiting there. Everyone I met tried to dissuade me from going, but having traveled so far just to do this one thing, I couldn't turn back.

Our first stop en route to Khost was Gardez, a place the aid worker who accompanied me grinningly called "dust town." Several hours after leaving Kabul and negotiating hairpin, mountainside turns, we reached the craggy village, which was indeed choked in a thick dust. Even with the vehicle's windows rolled up, all three of us had to lift handkerchiefs and scarves to our mouths. I was wearing a traditional chemise, as I'd been told clothing was very conservative in the area. I couldn't understand how people survived in Gardez. It was too dry to grow much and, other than the offices of a few NGOs and UN agencies, there didn't seem to be much of a commercial draw, although the main town was clogged with a lot of traffic and shops. Apparently there was a well-guarded U.S. military base a short drive away. I didn't expect Khost to be very different.

"The people here are proud of firing a gun or hunting in the mountains," Sartaj, the relief worker, explained to me as we pulled into his local office compound. "When they kill each other, you can ask them why did they do it, but no one can answer you. It may take three or four generations before the country really changes because this new generation is one of illiterates. In Kabul, they murder and steal from each other for no reason.

"The difference now with the Taliban gone is that the Russians came here, took money from the people, and killed civilians. They wanted us to carry the hashish across the border. The Americans haven't done that. They hurt the Taliban but don't kill the civilians. They are like our godfather."

On the drive I yearned for music other than the Hindi tapes the driver kept popping in. I supplied my own soundtrack in my head. We passed barely visible communities surrounded by high brick walls and phone piles with no lines, which were stolen during the war, while an unforgiving sun made the inside of the car feel like a microwave.

Unexpectedly I had to stay overnight in Gardez, as my escorts had work to take care of there. It was mind-numbingly boring. There was nothing to do but sit inside the sleeping quarters and look out the window as workers cooked or reconstructed a fallen building. There was no possibility of going outside the high-walled compound that surrounded us, so I napped periodically or watched Bollywood videos on an office worker's desktop computer. I also saw my first shooting star that evening and made a wish for my daughter, Mariela, so far away.

The next morning, we continued on to Khost.

INTO THE HOTBED

After arriving in Khost, I was greeted by Haji, the aid organization's local security chief. He was short and solidly built with light eyes.

"We are happy you have come so far to be here, without being forced," he said, greeting me with a handshake. "It is our pleasure and honor to help you find your story."

After a light lunch of soup and tea, I walked into the main part of the town to get a feel for the place. I was more than a little stir-crazy after the ride there and staying inside all day at Gardez. Walking through the teeming, loud streets of Khost city, I began to recall the journalists who were stoned to death in Mogadishu a decade before. As an antidote to my fear, I looked people right in the eye, smiled at kids, waved at stares, and took pictures. "Journalist, journalist!" some of the angrier adults heckled in English and Pashto. I didn't always know what they were saying, but I laughed with them. Rapidly moving through the crowded streets, often losing sight of my companion, a man who worked at the organization's compound, I also lost any sense of direction, as every person and every store began looking identical. I saw money changers, carpet sellers, tailors, street photographers offering to shoot portraits. I kept telling the man with me, "Make sure they know I'm a journalist and not a soldier. Make sure they know I'm not a soldier."

Suddenly it dawned on me how easy I would be to kill. Could I handle two, three, five of them? Maybe it would be someone from behind me? With a gun?

I began to feel that *anyone* could do something to me. With Nathan Ross Chapman in the back of my head, I expected a shot to ring out. Soldier, journalist, white, black—I wasn't from this place, and that's all that mattered. A lot of my black acquaintances who are writers or photographers feel that being black gets them a little bit further in such places. You're an American, a Westerner, but one who didn't exactly get all the promises that implies.

Without my noticing, twenty or thirty boys and men began following me. When I stopped to look at a photographer's Speedgraphic camera, I was surrounded. Someone started yelling in Pashto, and soon the majority of them joined in. Just when I felt that the tension in the air had reached its limit, a vehicle from the international organization with whom I was staying drove up. The office director hopped out of the backseat and came over, speaking something in Pashto that calmed everyone down. With him and the security chief there, I began to relax, not wanting to make a desperate dash for the car. Gently they guided me back to the vehicle, while the ever-watching crowd moved to the side of the road. After that, it was not-so-subtly conveyed to me that I would be safer staying inside, which meant a languorous day of taking notes, making lists, staring out a barred window, and daydreaming for hours. The frustration was gnawing at me, as random thoughts flooded my mind incessantly.

I've traveled half the world to find a killer. I spent too much money, time, and energy getting here. I am tired, burnt out, and feeling much the same as I did years ago, after returning from Sri Lanka, when I hit a mental wall and fell into despair and internalized darkness from sharing and hearing other people's pains.

Maybe my mother was right—maybe I came just to say that I had done it. I see the trip as one of solving a "case" and proving myself to myself. The very act of making it here, and back, would negate all the self-doubts, all the fears, all the sadness of what I lost or allowed to slip away. I have been so focused on trying to save other people's children that I haven't even made time to take care of my own child. But there is something else. Who am I to feel depressed or "traumatized" when it wasn't even me who was being victimized in these conflicts I've visited?

Two days later I was taken to meet the governor of Khost, a kindly, expatriate academic who had been asked to return shortly after the fall of the Taliban. Hakim Khan Taneewal had been away from Afghanistan in Pakistan and then Australia for twenty-three years, until he was appointed governor of Khost province in May 2002.

On the fading afternoon I went to visit, he sincerely appeared happy to see me. He said his prayers, and then we sat for more than an hour talking about my visit to Afghanistan and what he saw as the positive changes in Khost. Even though security was widely seen as having improved, Khost still had a bad reputation, particularly among the international community in Afghanistan. Nevertheless, Taneewal felt the best hope lay in the province's influx of educated people, open university, and free press. Highlighting what someone had told me in Kabul, he also noted that more than one hundred thousand Khost citizens lived throughout the world and sent remittances back to the community.

"Inside and outside Afghanistan, people have enmity with us," he noted. "With no telephone lines or Internet service, it means a sacrifice for people to come here, so they convince themselves to stay in Kabul or Herat. People fear Khost as a border province with Pakistan, but the Pashtun culture is changing. In the past, the Pashtun society had a regular anarchy. The tribes were autonomous, and the government presence was very weak. The national government let people live by their own codes, but with the Russian presence and the war in the '80s, tribal dynamics changed, and many people who were big in the city were not so important in the war. A new generation of commanders rose through the ranks, and many of them were poor. From the [mujaheddin] resistance and the communist-backed government, a 'Kalashnikov culture' prevailed. We are still trying to deal with it. When I first came back to Khost, I was like a prisoner."

Baka Khan Zadran was acting warlord at that point and controlled most legal income-generating activities throughout the province. In response, Taneewal enlisted the area's intellectuals and elders in a nonviolent brigade to force Zadran out.

"The Taliban was pushing *madrassas* and did not care for regular schools," said Taneewal. "The schools were operated by fees from the students, who had to pay the teachers' costs themselves. No high school was less than 2,700 to 3,500 Afghanis ($64 to $83). Today, we have over 120,000 girls and boys in school here. Despite the war, the people come and want their kids educated.

"Afghans have gone all over the world. They've seen other cultures and learned something, bringing back the good and the bad."

The following afternoon, it seemed that progress was being made. My impatience to meet Chapman's killer, his family, or anyone who knew anything about what had happened became obvious to my hosts, who scrambled to keep me occupied. Without my input, a decision was made by the security chief, a driver, my translators, and the head of the local office to take me out. Piling into a ridiculously tight SUV, we drove through the dust-choked town with the windows rolled up once again, staring at the pedestrians carrying rifles, who stared back at us. I thought about Governor Taneewal's description of a "Kalashnikov culture."

Nearly every man carried an AK–47. Surprisingly, it did not feel threatening, but more like an accessory. There was no "hearts and minds" campaign by American or international military forces to win over civilians in Khost, from what I saw. Unlike Kabul, where American and European personnel walked the streets interacting with children and their caregivers, there wasn't a foreign uniformed soldier in sight.

General Khail Baz was the Afghan army commander over Khost. Though he spoke no English whatsoever, we had an immediate cama-raderie. His office was extremely comfortable, almost ornate, with stuffed chairs, sofa, large wooden furniture, and wall paneling. He was compact, controlled, and (I would have bet) never perspired unless truly taxed. More than anything else, he exuded confidence, which is what I imagined one needed to oversee a region with Khost's recent history. He'd been there for sixteen months when we met.

"Mr. Taneewal was surrounded by all these different people running the government," he recalled. "Almost every day two to three people died. Children were kidnapped, schools shut down. Ordinary people who ran shops closed their businesses almost ten times a day because of insecu-rity. When we came in, an education center was soon opened. There were twelve districts in Khost province, and we asked about three hundred people to come help us. Padsha Khan was the only problem because he refused to cooperate."

On September 7, 2002, eight months since the death of Sergeant Nathan Ross Chapman after encountering Padsha Khan's soldiers on a desolate road, the warlord attacked the government in Khost. By the end of the day, General Baz's troops had overrun the warlord's positions and forced him to flee the city. From then on, the central government and Ta-neewal's government were allied, and because of the military success, Khail Baz was promoted to commander and then general of the Twenty-fifth Afghan Army Division based in Khost. Padsha Khan was arrested by forces of the central government in Kabul, and an agreement was reached with him so that he wouldn't interfere with the governmental administration of Khost from detention.

"From the military point of view, I see the future of Khost City as very bright," observed General Baz. "People want their kids to have education, but unfortunately 95 percent of them must sit out in the sun to do so. We hope that the international community takes this into consideration and helps the children who don't have proper schools. I think that Khost is a good example of security, if you compare it with the progress of other provinces in Afghanistan. Even President Karzai has said good things about the security in Khost, but many journalists come here and don't portray the real facts about it. These reports affect the unity of this country. Also, it would be extremely good if the Americans interacted with the people. People here are friendly and want to have better relations," he emphasized, leaning in close to me. "If the Americans don't learn and understand *Pashtunwali*, it will be difficult here for them." *Pashtunwali* is the Pashtun code of conduct, of honor. In conversations I'd had in the evenings while in Khost, I heard more than once that *Pashtunwali* would have been enough motivation for a teenage boy to kill an American soldier.

After visiting with General Khan, I asked to see the spot where Chapman had died. Reluctantly my Afghan companions agreed to drive to it, but warned that getting out of the vehicle was out of the question. We passed the ruins of a white mosque, a few yards from the side of the road. It had been hit by an American air strike on the first day of Ramadan, killing eighty people inside. Chapman had most likely visited the site just before his death.

I wasn't expecting the Afghanis to mark the spot where an American soldier had died, but I was still surprised when the driver stopped the truck abruptly and I saw that nothing gave the site away. It was at the beginning of a gentle, downward slope. On one side was what looked to be an abandoned building, and on the other was a dry, empty field. Just alongside the road a vendor was selling fruit underneath a large shade tree.

I couldn't help thinking that it seemed an unlikely place to die.

MISGUIDED YOUTH

The afternoon after my visit with General Khail Baz and to the spot where Sergeant Chapman died, a tribal religious leader came to the compound where I stayed to speak with me. He had known Chapman's killer and his family. More important, he knew what happened and why. Sitting in the front room, where I'd slept for three days on an array of pillows, I was greeted by the mullah, who wore a white chemise and black vest and had a long beard and dark red hair.

Initially nervous upon seeing me, he was escorted by one other man, and three members of my host organization sat with me in the room.

"I thought you might have been associated with Al-Qaeda, from your outfit," he said, smiling and pointing to my brown chemise, hat, and dark beard. "There are two major problems facing the youth here, a lack of education and infrastructure, and the opportunities for jobs. Jobs are very limited. We have a section of people who are getting depressed, smoking hashish and opium. Even if there are schools, the quality of the education or the teachers isn't always the best. Throughout the years, the mullahs were asking for *madrassas*, and the government wanted more schools. Now we want the schools to include a religious component to be taught side-by-side with a modern education of geography, math, science, and so forth."

At the time of my visit there were 150 *madrassas* in Khost, and the mullah with whom I met had attended the kind with a solely religious focus as well as those with both religious and practical education approaches. The mullahs like him who had lived in exile in Pakistan during the reign of the Taliban felt it was time to move beyond the old way of thinking. The newer mullahs were more intellectual, modern; some of them were even trained scientists. Not long after the war ended, a delegation of mullahs went to Kabul to see President Karzai and argue that there should be a separation of *madrassas* and schools.

"Discussion and debate do exist in *madrassas*," the red-haired mullah explained to me. "There is a strong relationship between the mullah and the *Taleb*. If education is expanded in this province, I assure you that problems with Al-Qaeda and the Taliban will not exist. There's a Pashto saying that goes, 'Don't kill an ignorant man, but kill his ignorance.' This is what we must do.

"Padsha Khan was in Khost at the time of this incident you ask about," he continued. "Khost wasn't stable like now. No one knows what happened to the boy. His cousin was taken by the Americans for eighteen months and then released. It was not a pre-planned attack. It was something the boy had heard to do. In the chaos that followed, the boy was able to flee and escape. The family was harassed by the government, and Padsha Khan put a lot of pressure on the family, the tribe, and the community to turn over the boy."

As the old man saw it, the young man was prepared to die. He saw the killing of Chapman as a suicide mission. Anyone who shoots an American soldier in broad daylight is going to expect to be killed. Many students of the *madrassas* or radical Islamic clerics believe that the best way to ascend to heaven is the one that is the easiest and fastest: dying while committing an act in the name of Islam. The fourteen-year-old shooter who took Nathan Chapman's life probably hadn't considered the possibility of continuing to live, much less getting away.

"When religion is explained to these people, you'll get killed and you go to heaven, or you'll get killed and you'll go to hell," noted the mullah.

"This is in their mind, so to get rid of it is difficult. The Taliban and Al-Qaeda twist your mind. They tell you, remind you that if you live, you'll grow old, you'll have no insurance, you'll work, you may be poor, etc."

The shooter didn't come from a broken family. In fact it was extraordinarily "normal": his father worked in town, and his mother cared for him, his cousins, and his grandparents. He was a typical village boy who experienced displacement and loss from the Americans' invasion of Afghanistan. After years of indoctrination by extreme religious leaders, he was primed. Youths like him grow up in refugee camps across the border in Pakistan or homeless inside Afghanistan. They see their families fight the Russians or other enemies of Islam, and they want to kill the enemies, too. If it means eighty members of your family go to heaven, why not kill an American?

"There is nothing in our religion that mandates killing or condones it," the mullah emphasized. "This boy heard something, believed it, and went to do this. I can tell you that a father lost his son. His mother developed tuberculosis. And his cousin spent two years in prison. A family has been destroyed. If you look at that time, every minute a plane was flying over your head, homes were being bombed, and there was a lot of noise and action. Initially, there was a feeling that this was like the Russians. Some very well-respected people, very honored people were taken and treated roughly. This made the community become defensive and angry.

"The first year the Americans were here, everybody was afraid of them," he continued. "What you see now is completely opposite of what it was. Americans would act on any hint of information, whether it was right or wrong. They were very heavy-handed. On the slightest rumor, they would bomb someone's house or make an arrest."

Matter-of-factly, the mullah told me that the boy's father lived a short distance from where I was staying. I knew if I pushed even a little, they would arrange the meeting with the boy's father, but it would have defeated the purpose of going there if some action I took caused problems for the people helping me, or worse, a blood feud. Chapman and the boy lost everything they were and everything they could have been. Chapman had gone to Afghanistan to avenge 9-11 and protect America. The boy who killed him had done so to avenge decades of family loss and death, to protect Islam, and ultimately to achieve a place greater than the one in which he existed.

I hadn't gotten everything I wanted, but I'd gotten more than I needed. I leaned back to catch the slow breeze coming through a window and listened to the mullahs speaking in rapid-fire tones to one another. Smiling broadly, I stared up at the thick wood beams in the ceiling and thought to myself, "Now I can go home."

WHEN A HERO DIES

Before leaving for Afghanistan, I had written a letter to Wilbur and Lynn Chapman, Nathan's parents, and managed to have one phone conversation with them at their home in Georgetown, Texas, near San Antonio. It was long after the media onslaught following their son's death, when TV trucks had invaded their small, close-knit community, adopting Nathan as the country's son for being the first to die fighting for the "American way of life." In contrast to Chapman, the first soldier to die in combat in Iraq, Marine Captain Ryan Anthony Beaupre, received a much quieter induction into the nation's collective memory. Sadly, his name seemed quickly forgotten by the public consciousness in that much-less-supported conflict.

I explained to the Chapmans why I was interested in Nathan's death, and as sympathetic as they were, I could tell the grief they felt over their lost son was still raw.

"It doesn't matter to me who killed my son, or why," Wilbur Chapman explained. "The fact is, he's dead."

The last time his parents and brother Keith saw Nathan alive was at Keith's Maryland wedding in August 2000. Nathan had been the best man and gave a moving toast, later dancing with his daughter, Amanda, just an infant then.

"I would wish you luck, but true marriage doesn't need luck," he told Keith and his new bride. "It needs love, honesty, and commitment, and those three things you have together. So I am going to close this out by saying that today is only the beginning. It only gets better from here."

Keith and his family watched the videotape of that toast and the rest of their wedding day on the night the news came about Nathan's death. It was a Friday and, coincidentally, Keith's birthday. Coming home from work late, he'd heard on the radio about the first American casualty lost to hostile fire in Afghanistan.

"I felt that there were hundreds of men and women like him who were taking similar risks, so it left my mind," recalled Keith to me. "My wife met me at the door and came into the garage as I was parking. She told me that she had bad news, but there was nothing on her face that betrayed anything. I may have thought, She burned my birthday cake or something. Then she said, 'Your father called.' My reaction was one not of incredulity—it was like, 'He was the one.' Those were the words I used. Out of all the people that were over there at this time, he was the one. Looking back, I wondered how it would have been different if he were the second, or tenth, or hundredth. Would I, we, have been less prepared?"

His body was flown from Afghanistan, via a U.S. Army base in Landstuhl, Germany, and he was buried at Takoma National Cemetery in Kent, Washington, following a service in his honor at Fort Lewis, his home base for much of a decade-long career with Company C in the Third Battalion of the First Special Forces Group. Memorial services were also held in Ohio at his graduating high school in Centreville and his parents' home in Texas. Posthumously he was awarded a Purple Heart and Bronze Star, among other commendations. A cul-de-sac at Fort Lewis was bestowed with his name.

"A lot of people applied to become a Green Beret or seek out that training, but only a small fraction make it in," noted Keith. "That was lost on me until after his death and we attended ceremonies. The number of medals he received, I had nothing to compare it with, but my father told me it was an unusual number of medals for the years of service he had. Back then, I don't know if it was so much overwhelming, as I was unprepared to speak about it. The more I learned about what he was doing and why he was there, and what brought men like him to that place, that I feel like that was something that I'm proud to have a brother involved in. You never know how many risks he took in the days leading up to that one."

Somehow I believed that if the world could figure out how to keep children and youth from fighting wars, then perhaps it wouldn't be so difficult to stop adults. I certainly didn't find all the answers, but I know they lie within the stories and experiences of young people such as the unforgettable ones I met while researching this book and the thousands more like them who too often remain faceless, and nameless.

NOTES

1. Victoria Garcia, "U.S. Military Assistance to 1460 Report Countries: 1990–2005," Center for Defense Information, April 12, 2004.

2. Center for Emerging Threats and Opportunities, "Child Soldiers: Implications for U.S. Forces," Seminar Report CETO 005–02, Marine Corps Warfighting Laboratory, November 2002.

3. "People on War: Country Report Afghanistan," by Greenberg Research, Inc., for the International Committee of the Red Cross Worldwide Consultation on the Rules of War, November 1999, p. 11.

Acknowledgments

THE MOST IMPORTANT JOURNEYS in life should not be taken alone, and this book was no exception. Countless individuals held my hand, pushed me from behind, led the way, or just walked next to me for various stretches. In crossing the finish line I carry them with me, as well as my ancestors' lifeline of hope. That hope is embodied in the memories of individuals such as my grandfather Lester McCombs, a World War II veteran who died on my thirty-fifth birthday while I was reporting in Afghanistan, and my great-grandmother Mattie King, who lived to see a century's worth of stories, and then some.

Without question I would not have been able to complete this book were it not for the understanding and support of Jeanette Vera. Despite the rocky route of our relationship, she never allowed me to doubt myself or the inevitable fruition of this project. More important, she kept the bond between our daughter and me alive, often when I was not available to do it myself.

My family in St. Louis, Missouri, including my parents, Jimmie and Myrtis Briggs, and my brother, Thomas, have always been a bedrock.

Despite their perpetual anxiety over my well-being, they've backed me up emotionally and spiritually when I needed it. They are my best home team. Likewise, my closest friends since childhood, Rod Burton and Landon Reid, have remained pillars of integrity, strength, honor, and friendship throughout my life.

The bulk of financial and networking support for this project came from the Open Society Institute (OSI) in New York through the Individual Project Fellowship. Its former director, Gail Goodman, is someone whom I am blessed to call a friend. At OSI, I also thank George Soros and Aryeh Neier, to whom I owe a great debt, as well as Claudia Hernandez, Erlin Ibreck, and Whitney Johnson. Other funders to whom I am extremely grateful include the Fund for Investigative Journalism, the Bronx Council on the Arts, the National Association of Black Journalists, the Dick Goldensohn Fund, and Margaret Engel at the Alicia Paterson Foundation.

Special thanks go out to Penny Abeywardena, Stephen Ferry, Henrik Haggstrom, Richard Petro, Peter Vrooman, Chuck Hirshberg, and Sarah Wells, who graciously took the time not only to read rough drafts but to provide valuable opinions and reactions. I have incredible appreciation of their energy and integrity. Early in my career, Rich forever became a *compadre* during our time in the *Washington Post* mailroom.

I am grateful for the opportunity to do this book and must thank Jo Ann Miller at Basic Books, my dogged and committed agent Eileen Cope at Lowenstein & Associates, and especially Linda Carbone for their patience, honesty, and refusal to let me fail. I also want to thank Raquel Cepeda, Victoria Valentine, Betsy Gleick, Elinor Tatum, and Holly Hughes for supporting my writing through assignments.

As my commitment, focus, and energy for this book waned, which was too often, a family of friends and colleagues helped carry the load, which was a gift I cannot forget. Thank you especially to Eduardo and Gloria

Vera, Lourdes Rivera, Ashley Henriquez, Jodi Eastman, Susan Patricof, Neyda Martinez, Fernando Ramirez, Belinda DeJesus, David Yaffe, Hatice Nazan, Hilary Duffy, Liz Gilbert, Mariella Furrer, Martina Muehlegg, Darwin Brown, Daniela Wuerz, Michelle Olofson, Cleve Lamison, Alexandra Huster, Johnny Drake, Fabrizio and Leslie Di Mitri, Christa Sanders, Mercedes Doretti, Pedro Linger Gasiglia, Beverlee Bruce, Ruth Morris, Nicole Sealey, Kendall Moore, Krishan Trotman, David Friend, Claudia Dowling, Bi Karanja, David Poplack, Steve O'Malley, Nancy Lucas, Alexandra Posada, Thomas Arnhardt, Steve Jones, Marieke Van Woerkem, Kristina Nassen, Susan Watts, Brian Palmer, Gerard Gaskin, Bianca Bockman, Rachel Cobb, Sherine Xavier, Julia Shaw, Colleen Malone, Jasmine Jaquez, Jay O. Sanders, and Marcia Davis for your empowering support.

Scores of organizations assisted in my research at home and reporting from the field, and in particular I thank the following individuals for their assistance and generosity, including Gillian Caldwell and the staff of WITNESS; Henrik Haggstrom at Radda Barnen and the members of the International Save the Children Alliance; Jo Becker, Joanne Mariner, Corinne Dufka, Peter Bouckaert, and Veronica Matusha of Human Rights Watch; Rachel Stohl at the Center for Defense Information; the members of the Coalition to Stop the Use of Child Soldiers; Saudamini Siegrist, Nicole Toutounji, and Jehane Sedky at UNICEF; Yvonne Acosta in the United Nation Secretary-General's office; Olara Otunnu; Charlie Borchini at CETO; Betty Bigombe at the World Bank; Kris Torgeson at Medecins Sans Frontières/Doctors Without Borders USA; Mike Wessells with Christian Children's Fund; the staff at USAID; Jane Lowicki, Allison Pillsbury, Sarah Spencer, Julia Freedson, and Marie de la Soudiere with the International Rescue Committee/Women's Commission for Refugee Women and Children; Eric and Raymond in Rwanda; Rommel Rojas and the staff at Bienestar Familiar; the staff and children at the

Butterfly Garden; Ibrahim Sesay with UNICEF in Afghanistan; Susanne Schmeidel and the staff of Swiss Peace; the kids with Seeds of Peace in Kabul, Afghanistan; Aloys Habimana and LIPRODHOR; the staffs of World Vision International, GUSCO, and St. Mary's College in Uganda; Martin and the members of the Cacique Nutibara in Medellín; the Comboni Missionaries; Marcy Auguste; the families of the Concerned Parents Association; and the Liberation Tigers of Tamil Eelam.

For allowing me to enter their lives and attempt to capture their stories weeks, months, and years at a time, I am eternally thankful to François Minani, Angelina Acheng Atyam, Sr. Rachele Fassera, Sebastiana Figerardo, Keith, Wilbur, and Lynn Chapman, Gueso, Duilio, and Luís. I pray you find the truth and sincerity in my words.

Finally, there are a group of individuals whose presence in my life is something I recognize and honor daily. Most are colleagues, and all are kindred spirits who have remained desperately needed confidants, drinking buddies, and movie mates. During moments of drift or rootlessness, they are my anchors. Joe Rodriguez is more committed to social uplift than nearly anyone I know, at times a father-figure, a brother-figure, but always a friend. Lacy Austin at the International Center of Photography is a phenomenal bundle of love who continues to show me the true meaning of compassion and selflessness. It's hard to know what I can write about Andre Lambertson, Russell Frederick, and Clarence Williams, other than the fact they are my "found" brothers, who keep my feet moving when I think I'm too tired. My love for them is limitless. The importance of Damaso Reyes's camaraderie, support, and friendship to my daughter, Mariela, and me cannot be overestimated, and I am grateful. Marina Hoffman is a spirit who defies definition. Incredibly thoughtful and nurturing, she remains one of the most dependable people around me. Misha Arguetty is a soulmate and confidant whom I am blessed to know.

I would never have taken the steps to become a journalist were it not for three key individuals: Travis Allen, Johnette Stubbs, and Ray Villaman. Memories of sharing a room with Travis at Morehouse College provide badly needed laughs, and it was he who first suggested I explore the possibilities of writing. I will always claim the Stubbs family in Maryland and Virginia as my own. Their strength and love have been an endless fountain to which I've never been denied access. Johnette, Johnnie, Lavette, Mark, and Aretha walk with me. When it comes to generosity, Ray Villaman and his wife, Christine, always have an abundance of it. It was Ray with whom I made the first big step, to Washington, D.C., and the last steps on the book were with their help.

Bibliography

Barnitz, Laura, Jimmie Briggs, Frank Smyth, and Rachel Stohl. "Colombia: No Safe Haven from War." Youth Advocate Program International Resource Paper. July 11, 2001.

Center for Emerging Threats and Opportunities. "Child Soldiers: Implications for U.S. Forces," Seminar Report CETO 005–02. Marine Corps Warfighting Laboratory. November 2002.

Des Forges, Allison. *"Leave None to Tell the Story": Genocide in Rwanda*. New York: Human Rights Watch, 1999.

Ehrenreich, Rosa. *The Scars of Death: Children Abducted by the Lord's Resistance Army in Uganda*. New York: Human Rights Watch, 1997.

Garcia, Victoria. "U.S. Military Assistance to 1460 Report Countries: 1990–2005." Center for Defense Information. April 12, 2004.

Gersony, Robert. *The Anguish of Northern Uganda: Results of a Field-Based Assessment of the Civil Conflicts in Northern Uganda*. Kampala, Uganda: USAID Mission, 1997.

Greenberg Research, Inc. "People on War." International Committee of the Red Cross Worldwide Consultation on the Rules of War. 1999.

Machel, Graça. *The Impact of War on Children: A Review of Progress since the 1996 United Nations Report on the Impact of Armed Conflict on Children*. New York: Palgrave, 2001.

Nowrojee, Binaifer. *Shattered Lives: Sexual Violence during the Rwandan Genocide and Its Aftermath.* New York: Human Rights Watch, 1996.

Rakita, Sara, and Yoden Thonden. *Lasting Wounds: Consequences of Genocide and War for Rwanda's Children.* New York: Human Rights Watch, 2003.

Rosenberg, Tina. *Children of Cain: Violence and the Violent in Latin America.* New York: Penguin, 1992.

Rosenblatt, Roger. *Children of War.* New York: Anchor, 1983.

U.S. State Department. Country Reports on Human Rights Practices, 2000. Bureau of Democracy, Human Rights, and Labor. 2001.

SOURCES OF INTEREST

Amnesty International: http://web.amnesty.org/pages/childsoldiers-index-eng

Center for Defense Information: http://www.cdi.org

The Children and Armed Conflict Unit: http://www.essex.ac.uk/armedcon

Child Rights Information Network: http://www.crin.org

Coalition to Stop the Use of Child Soldiers: http://www.child-soldiers.org

Human Rights Watch: http://www.hrw.org/campaigns/crp/index.htm

Reuters AlertNet: http://www.alertnet.org

UNICEF: http://www.unicef.org

United Nations Integrated Regional Information Networks: http://www.irinnews.org

War Child: http://www.warchild.org

Watchlist on Children and Armed Conflict: http://www.watchlist.org

Index